Buns, Bails an

A season watching c

By David Spiller

Welcome to Grace Road (Photo: Peter David Lush)

1903659035 1 912 3F *ONS Ltd.*

Buns, Bails and Banter

A season watching county cricket

A CIP catalogue record for this book is available from the British Library.

First published in Great Britain in May 2001 by:
London League Publications Ltd.
P.O. Box 10441, London E14 0SB

ISBN: 1-903659-03-5

Cover design by:

Layout:

Printed and bound by:

Foreword

Buns, Bails and Banter gives its readers some refreshing new angles on a familiar subject - the county cricket championship. This competition remains the central feature of the first class cricket season. I enjoy immensely all the forms of cricket we play, including the pressure situations created by one-day cricket, but I think that given the choice between them I would still prefer to make a century in the championship.

The 2000 season was the first featuring the new, two-division championship. For the players this had both pluses and minuses. It meant that all of the games we played were important to us, and it made every point vital. On the debit side there were probably not enough good games of cricket. Teams were less inclined to gamble, and more inclined to go for bowling and batting points. It may be that we shall eventually see a re-introduction of first innings points in the four-day game.

It is good to see favourable comment on the commitment of county cricketers. The Leicestershire players are extremely proud of playing for their county, and their work levels are very high, during the matches themselves, and also pre-season. If the team has an off day, we feel it badly.

Few supporters see all of their team's matches, home and away, but of course the players get used to travelling and spending time away from home - and this is when the team atmosphere is especially important. It was good to recall Leicestershire's win at Southampton, achieved without any of the county's front-line bowlers, in what was probably the best game of cricket we played in during the Summer. I was less happy to be reminded of the defeat at Guildford, a game where we held our own with the eventual county champions for nearly two days, only for our batting to be swept away on the second evening.

Taking all the county grounds into consideration, I love playing at Grace Road. Not too many teams enjoy taking us on there. (Maybe our reputation is a bit like the old football reputation of Wimbledon.) It is not only that Grace Road is 'home' to me. The ground has really excellent facilities, with good outdoor nets, and a superb indoor school. The groundsmen work very hard, the catering is good, and the whole enterprise is very much a team effort. Outside of Grace Road I always enjoy playing at Lords, and it was one of the drawbacks of the two-division format that we did not play a game there in 2000.

One of the nice aspects of first class cricket - much less common in football - is the relative closeness of players and spectators in the grounds. I think Leicestershire manages to attract a fair range of different people to its matches, though the four-day game is always likely to appeal in the main to retired spectators and hospitality guests. The one-dayers offer a lot of opportunities for attracting youngsters to grounds. An attractive feature of the Leicester environment is the variety of successful teams from different sports - cricket, football, rugby union, and so on. We often get people coming to Grace Road in the morning, going on to watch the Leicester Tigers rugby union team in the afternoon, and returning for the evening session at Grace Road.

Problems with the weather are endemic to county cricket, and were worse than usual in 2000. Players probably get more used to them than spectators. We have no card players in the Leicestershire team, so on a bad day players tend to go off to the gym or the indoor school, or watch some TV. Spectators have fewer options open to them when the rain falls.

I get 100% enjoyment from playing cricket. A lot of people may be unfortunate enough to get up in the morning and not particularly look forward to their day. As cricketers we have a fantastic life, and I feel honoured to be captaining Leicestershire's first class cricket team, and participating in the sort of matches reported in *Buns, Bails and Banter*.

Vince Wells.
March 2001. Vince Wells is the captain of Leicestershire CCC.

Acknowledgements
The author would like to thank:
Peter David Lush, Dave Farrar and Michael O'Hare for congenial editing of the book, and for providing the statistical information and additional photographs.
Sylvia Michael, Hon Archivist at Leicestershire CCC, for her kind help in identifying photographs, and permission to use her own photographs.
John Holland LRPS DPAGB, for permission to use photographs of Taunton.
Terry Mahoney Photographic Services, for permission to use the photograph of Canterbury.
James Bailey, Durham CCC, for permission to use the photograph of Chester-le-Street by Ian Dobson Photography.
Neville Chadwick Photography for photographs of Grace Road.
Jenny Spiller for thinking of the title *Buns, Bails and Banter*.
Robin Osmond for reading and commenting on an early draft of the book.

Introduction

The Millennium did not, as some appeared to expect, usher in some new Age of Aquarius, but it does appear to have persuaded our sporting administrators to change the apparently immutable. Within a few months of the one changing to two at the start of the year, Rugby Union's 90-year old Five Nations had become Six and the still more venerable county cricket championship had undergone the most dramatic change in its history, moving to two divisions with promotion and relegation between them.

On the opening day of the 2000 season Gloucestershire played Sussex. The two counties have been meeting for as long as the championship has been played (exactly how long this is depends on who you ask - 1864, 1873 and 1890 all have their proponents). Neither, if like *Wisden Cricketers' Almanack* you accept 1890 as the starting date, has ever won the championship - although Sussex have been runners-up six times. Yet they had started every previous season with the theoretical possibility of becoming champions. In 2000, as Second Division teams, they had to win promotion - something neither achieved - in order to regain this possibility.

This profound shift reflected concern over the state of English cricket, and in particular the poor results achieved by the England team in the 1990s. Numerous potential villains have been indicted for this decline, and by the late 1990s a consensus for the prosecution gathered around the championship and its alleged profusion of purposeless, inconsequential cricket.

It is undoubtedly right that we should question the purpose of our institutions, however venerable they may be. The county game has been the basic currency of the English game since the 1860s and 1870s when it saw off the alternative structure provided by the travelling XIs of the age. In that time all of the greatest English players have played the bulk of their first-class careers in the championship - the nearest thing to an exception was SF Barnes, but even he played a couple of seasons with Lancashire - and since 1968 they have been joined, at one time or another, by most of the world's greatest players.

Many immensely distinguished careers have been conducted almost entirely in the championship. As a Glamorgan fan I can point to Alan Jones and Don Shepherd, respectively scorer of the most first-class runs and taker of most first-class wickets without playing test cricket. Leicestershire can claim heroes like George Geary, JH King and Ewart Astill who did play for England, but whose fame was local and based upon decades of dedicated service to their county.

The county championship is part of the fabric of our national life. It no longer attracts the huge crowds it once did, particularly in the post-war years when all spectator sports boomed. David Spiller's year with Leicestershire casts him as a member of a distinct minority, one with more than its share of idiosyncrasies and eccentricities. Yet there is little doubt that it retains a large passive following of fans who still identify with their county. The broadsheet newspapers still regard the county game as a staple of their summer sports coverage. The success of a website like *Cricinfo* in part reflects this continuing interest. Many more people than attend the matches would miss the competition if it were suddenly not there.

This decline as a paying spectator sport has created pressure on the competition. If it were as well supported as before, it would have little need to justify itself and could claim to be an end in itself. The problem is that it does not do so. County clubs are subsidised by payments from the England and Wales Cricket Board, derived from the profits made by test matches. Little wonder that many draw the conclusion that its primary, some would say sole, purpose is to help generate a successful England team and when it fails to do so regard it as culpable for that failure. Jibes about "pie-throwing" from our more successful rivals down under only serve to reinforce the indictment - although it is worth noting that since Rodney Marsh indulged in that famous piece of intercontinental sledging the Australian Cricket Board has been delighted to allow its players, including in 2001 Daniel Marsh, son of Rodney, who will be playing for Leicestershire - to supplement their experience, averages and incomes by playing in England.

Much comment has been frankly hysterical. It would be possible to conclude from some comment from sources that frankly ought to know better that, instead of being English cricket's most dedicated supporters, the county clubs and their membership are a long-running conspiracy to ensure that England are pinned to the lower reaches of the International Cricket Council's newly-created world league. When Mike Atherton, whose comments on the game are normally as well-considered as his innings for England, drew a wholly negative picture of the county game, it was hardly surprising that many county fans pointed to his willingness to draw a lucrative (and entirely deserved) benefit from the system for which he had so little time.

The decline in live support is also an international phenomenon afflicting the Ranji Trophy and what was once the Sheffield Shield (those of us who cherish the county championship can at least be grateful that it has not been insulted in the manner of the Shield's transformation into the Pura Milk trophy), suggesting that there is little the game's rulers could have done over half a century of decline to arrest the problem.

The complaints about inconsequential cricket are harder to answer. But as David Spiller points out this is partly due to the disruptive effect of the weather. That cricket can take five days, and still end in a draw, is one of the many facets that makes it incomprehensible to many not brought up with the game. But that leisurely time frame and vulnerability to the elements provide the game with its variety, unpredictability and subtlety - characteristics prized by its followers.

Perhaps the most serious indictment is that while full-time professionals invariably dominate part-time performers, however gifted, in other sports, the longest-standing and most extensive full-time professional set-up in cricket has been unable to generate test teams capable of consistently beating opposition composed in part or full of part-timers.

The aim of the two-division system is to ensure that county teams play more meaningful games, involving players in issues of promotion and relegation deep into the season. The evidence from season one is inconclusive - Division Two ended in a cavalry charge with almost every team still in contention to the final week, but Surrey's domination of Division One and the early emergence of a clear relegation trio showed that competitiveness cannot be legislated into existence.

The suspicion remains that there is a subtext to the changes, with the aim being to reduce the number of counties. The three-up, three-down system was designed to allay the fears of more vulnerable counties, but one wonders how long it will be before the more powerful players start complaining of insecurity and agitating for a reduction to two, one, or even an end of season playoff. Mark Ramprakash's request for a transfer and move to Surrey in order to further his England ambitions may have been a convenient rationalisation to escape a county-player relationship which had gone sour, but also felt like a straw in the wind.

The medium-term impact of the central contracts system, another innovation in 2000, on the championship remains to be seen. Current England players play little part in David Spiller's narrative, which is dominated by the solid county performer and overseas players. Darren Gough's decision to move his home from Yorkshire to the home counties and Nasser Hussain's Essex tally of 41 runs were both expressions of rapidly-growing detachment. It all rather begged the question of what purpose there is in counties developing potential test players if they are to be almost totally lost as soon as they reach the requisite standard. Increasingly it appears that the ideal county employee will be the player who is an above-average county performer but falls just short of test standard - precisely the sort of player in whom Leicestershire (at least in the eyes of the England selectors) have specialised over the last few seasons.

What does seem certain is that the championship will survive in some shape or form. Advocates of a competition based around city teams are missing a very basic point - that all sporting allegiance is based on identification built up over time. To call your team Leeds or London rather than Yorkshire or Middlesex won't revitalise interest in cricket any more than Leeds Rugby Union or the London Broncos Rugby League club have been able to pull in big audiences.

Among the assets of county cricket is the sense of continuity that links Jack Russell to W.G. Grace, Michael Vaughan to Maurice Leyland and Vince Wells to Ewart Astill (it would be unfair to suggest that the same spectators are involved). That sort of identity is vitally important, and cannot be built overnight.

David Spiller has provided a fan's-eye view of this game at one of its decisive turning points. He has chronicled its idiosyncrasies, its humour, the commitment of its performers and its chronic failings - most damningly the game's dismissive treatment of the casual paying spectator.

For this reason it should retain its interest for some time. It would be no surprise if it were to be read with interest by cricket fans in 10, 20 or even 50 years - still less if the game those readers is watching still features a county championship as its central professional structure.

Huw Richards
Walthamstow, February 2001.

Huw Richards is the cricket correspondent of the *International Herald Tribune*, and also writes widely on rugby union, rugby league and football

About the author

David Spiller has retired twice - from the British Council, and from a small research unit at Loughborough University - and is now fulfilling a lifelong ambition of watching a great deal of cricket, and sometimes writing about it. He moved to Leicestershire four years ago, and (like all late converts to anything) has become passionate about the county's cricket club. His left arm slow deliveries once took 5 for 0 for his school house third team, though two of his victims could not hold a bat. He is married with two sons; his wife, Gaynor Barton, has never been to a cricket match, but he is grateful to her for drawing his attention to London League Publications.

Interested in sport?

London League Publications are a specialist sports and hobbies publisher. To order our free book-list, send a stamped addressed envelope to the address below.

Our rugby league magazine, *Our Game*, is of interest to anyone who follows that sport, or is interested in sports history. To order a copy of the latest issue, send a cheque for £2.00 to the address below.

(Cheques to London League Publications Ltd, no credit card orders).
London League Publications Ltd, PO Box 10441, London E14 0SB.

Preface

This book records a spectator's thoughts on an English county cricket season. I set out to watch all of Leicestershire's four-day matches - home and away - in Division One of the English County Championship for the year 2000. Until this season my view of first-class cricket was largely conditioned by Test matches on television, with all their high-profile players, slow-motion replays, technical devices and comment from the experts. Watching county matches from beyond the boundary ropes is a very different experience. The following reports are well-informed, I hope, but they are not dominated by technical detail of the kind relayed so capably in books by players or professional commentators. In its place I describe from a spectator's viewpoint the wealth of fascinating incident which cannot find a place in the brief, daily newspaper reports of county cricket. How do the cricketing celebrities perform on the county stage? What is contributed by the bit-part players? What are players' foibles and curious mannerisms? What characterises the different county grounds? At which grounds (amazingly) could I not buy a sandwich? What do spectators say to each other? How do the umpires add to the fun? What happens when it rains?

The county scene provides a welcome antidote to the grimly competitive stuff of Test cricket. County players and spectators take their cricket seriously, to be sure, but there are also many hilarious incidents to describe in a season.

That this was the first year's cricket in the third millennium, and the first year of the new, two-division championship, gave it additional interest. I wanted to see how the new championship format would work, and also whether press reports of listless, uncommitted county players were justified? Watching a good county side - Leicestershire - throughout their programme, allowed me to see how one team responded to the ups and downs of a season, and how individual players fluctuated during the year. Experiencing a number of different county grounds, and the facilities which they did, and did not, offer was an eye-opener, and provided further evidence about the survival chances of county cricket.

I hope the book will shed light upon a scene which is not always visited by those keen on cricket, and will entertain anyone interested in the game.

David Spiller.
April 2001.

President : Christopher Martin-Jenkins.
Chairman : David Allsop CBE

The Cricket Society

Join a group that offers so much of interest to all those who care about cricket.

Meetings, Talks, Dinners, Quizzes, Journals, Newsletters, Library, Awards, Shop and a cricket team.

- Formed in 1945 we have over 2,000 members in the UK and around the world. Well known cricket personalities from all aspects of the game speak at regular meetings in London, Bath, Birmingham and Chester-le-Street.
- Spring and Autumn Dinners are held in London with other dinners in Birmingham, Bath and Chester-le-Street
- We publish twice a year the critically acclaimed Journal with original articles by writers familiar and new.
- The News Bulletin appears eight times a year with information on all The Society's activities.
- Each year The Society makes a range of Awards to cricketers from schools and first class cricket plus a Book of the Year award.
- Members may borrow books from the comprehensive library. A postal video library is also available.
- The Cricket Society Trust is a registered charity providing funds for the advancement of remedial training and physical education for people disabled or deprived by social or economic circumstances.
- The Society Cricket XI is drawn from members all over the country and play about 30 matches per season against a varied selection of opponents.
- An annual quiz is held in London for the Callow Cup.
- A Cricketers' Service is held each year in St John's Wood Church.
- The Society offers ties and other reasonably priced merchandise including an exclusive Christmas card each year.

Annual Membership is only £13 (with a reduced rate of £9 for Senior Citizens).
To join The Society or to obtain further information please contact:
The Cricket Society, PO Box 6024, Leighton Buzzard, LU7 7ZS.

Or visit www.cricsoc.cricket.org

Contents

		Page
1.	Derbyshire versus Leicestershire	1
2.	Lancashire versus Leicestershire	13
3.	Leicestershire versus Somerset	23
4.	Leicestershire versus Hampshire	37
5.	Durham versus Leicestershire	41
6.	Yorkshire versus Leicestershire	51
7.	Leicestershire versus Derbyshire	59
8.	Leicestershire versus Surrey	65
9.	Leicestershire versus Durham	77
10.	Surrey versus Leicestershire	87
11.	Kent versus Leicestershire	97
12.	Hampshire versus Leicestershire	105
13.	Leicestershire versus Yorkshire	117
14.	Leicestershire versus Lancashire	123
15.	Somerset versus Leicestershire	135
16.	Leicestershire versus Kent	139
Conclusion: County Cricket 2000		141
Appendix 1: The Leicestershire Players		145
Appendix 2: Statistics		149

In the match scores: * = captain, + = wicket-keeper.

1. Derbyshire versus Leicestershire
Derby - County Ground, 26 to 29 April

Thursday, 27 April, 2000. On the first day of cricket's new, two-division County Championship, I arrived at the Derbyshire cricket ground 15 minutes before play was scheduled to begin. Technically, this was the *second* day, because on Wednesday play had been abandoned, at Derby and at all the other five scheduled championship matches. It was the first time cancellations had occurred on this scale for 25 years. So here, already, was the first bugbear for the English cricket fan: the weather. This morning the rain had stopped, but the ground lay chilled under a dome of low, grey cloud, and a bitter wind swept across the unprotected stands.

Derby! Finding a way to the ground from the railway station is just the start of a visitor's troubles. It is bordered - indeed the whole of Derby seems to be bordered - by dual carriageways bearing continuous heavy traffic, the grind and roar of which is a constant companion to the cricket. Today this was augmented by the louder roar of bulldozers clearing a large space behind the grandstand - reportedly preparing for a leisure centre on land leased out by the cricket club.

A clump of unsightly brick buildings are dumped at random along part of the cricket ground's perimeter, next to a stretch of grass bank surmounted by a line of flimsy-looking trees. Next come the most popular banks of seating, albeit uncovered, and then an enclosed but empty wooden structure without seats - apparently the remnants of an old pavilion, now disused. Behind this area is a derelict yard from which three small boys were climbing over a wire fence into the ground.

Because this was the first proper day of the season, there was much greeting and hello-ing in the members' building, which my Leicestershire season ticket entitled me to enter. At 11 am - the time scheduled for play to start - I counted 30 people here, and another 54 scattered around the ground (with perhaps a few more concealed in crevices). Most of those present were over 60, though a couple of children were in the members' area, looking bemused: "Is this Derbyshire, dad?" A touching exchange took place between a grandfather and grandson, each checking that the other was not feeling cold. But in the whole three days of this match I saw very few spectators between the ages of 20 and 40.

1

It was clear that play would not be starting promptly, and I moved out of the cramped members' seating to walk around the playing area. That wind, notorious on the Derbyshire ground, was living up to its reputation, and the few people not under cover were badly exposed. The ground's seating for non-members is particularly basic. The only covered option is a six-row bank of plastic chairs in a brick construction with a corrugated iron roof. Today this had one incumbent. The other possibility was to park the car on a soggy stretch of ground in front of the grass bank, and a few drivers had already done this. They were mostly slumbering behind the wheel, but six fearless people had drawn easy chairs from their car boots and were seated at the perimeter fence. Padded overcoats, rugs and flasks were much in evidence, and one man sensibly wore a Russian-style fur hat. Another, convinced by the date that summer had arrived, was holding a sandwich, and had a large jar of pickled onions open in front of him (this at 11.15am). A lady was hard at work knitting a cardigan, as if in urgent need of the extra clothing.

After an 11.30am pitch inspection, there was another announcement: play would begin at 12.15pm, and Leicestershire had won the toss and chosen to field. And so - since play had not begun in any of the other matches around the country - the first ball of the new century's County Championship was bowled at Derby just after midday.

That first ball was from the Leicestershire fast bowler James Ormond, and went through to the wicket-keeper, watched by the batsman; as did four of Ormond's remaining five balls in the first over. The nine other fielders looked on. A visitor from outer space, making a first visit to an English cricket match, might at this point have asked a question about the purpose of the game.

Play before lunch featured an unusual case of mistaken identity. The opening batsmen had been announced as Stephen Stubbings and Michael DiVenuto. There was some unproductive prodding and poking from these two for 10 overs, until "DiVenuto" played on to one of the few deliveries from Ormond that needed bat to be put to ball. He departed, followed by an announcement that the batsman out was in fact Mathew Dowman, and not - "as previously announced" - DiVenuto. The real DiVenuto came to the wicket, and almost immediately celebrated his early-season reprieve with three runs to mid-wicket, soon followed by a boundary through point from an extravagant stroke. An old chap sitting in front of me said "Now we *know* it's not Dowman, don't we?"

Just before lunch Stubbings joined his fellow opener in the pavilion. He had hit a couple of boundaries off Philip DeFreitas, but was then wonderfully caught by Stevens, diving and taking the ball low at short square leg. A lone spectator near the grandstand leapt to his feet, and let rip a shrill, ranting stream of invective which echoed shockingly across the ground, and over the heads of the silent Derbyshire faithful, huddled in their seats. "A Leicestershire supporter," said one, witheringly, as if no other explanation was needed. It was not until I visited Leicestershire's home ground at Grace Road that I was to discover the identity of this enthusiast.

Lunch was taken at 44 for 2, not a moment too soon for renewing circulation of the blood. I made for the small refreshment hut, which was the only indoor refuge for non-members. Seating comprised half-a-dozen tables, and a bench along the front of the building, where patrons could nurse a cup of tea and watch the cricket. A few feet from the rear windows, the bulldozer bucked and ground away furiously. Its roar swept through the hut, obliterating attempts at conversation. The three doors in the hut were all wedged open, to ensure that the wind could sweep across the room, and the noise of the bulldozer could be heard to best effect.

The refreshments service was run by a woman engaged in a violent argument with a young male colleague. The queue was mostly served by a flustered, elderly lady who - a bloke at my table observed - had "come to catering late in life". A single copy of the menu, much in demand, was spattered with elements of several meals eaten on previous occasions. The food itself made me think of a transport cafe. (Special today: chips, £1.20.) Surprisingly, Leicestershire's general manager, James Whitaker, was in the hut, tucking into a bacon butty and looking absurdly fit and youthful among the other rheumy-eyed occupants, few of us under 65.

Several of the customers tackling 'big breakfasts' and other delights were on nodding acquaintance with each other, though their exchanges were on the restrained side.

"All right, Arthur?" "Pushing on. You?" "Bearing up under the strain."

I talked a bit with someone at my table - an agreeable chap who would not see 75 again. I said that the forecast had promised a better day. "It never is at Derby," he replied cheerfully.

3

These exchanges typified, I thought, the Derbyshire supporter's outlook: knowledgeable; dour, but full of pawky humour; inured to hardship, and not expecting anything more; disgruntled, yet (I was to find) fiercely loyal. They exemplified the view, held by some user-survey gurus, that there is little point in asking customers about service quality, because customers get used to what they have always had. The club's annual subscription is £90 - a figure only exceeded, among other counties, by Surrey, Sussex, Lancashire and Durham. Of Derbyshire's immediate neighbours, the Nottinghamshire subscription is £70, and Leicestershire £43, both for better services than the pitiful offerings at the County Ground. I commented on this to a regular visitor, who said, again with that air of placid acceptance: "Aye, Derby's always been expensive".

Yet the Derbyshire membership figures seem to tell a story. This year they have 2,000 members - down 900 on the previous season, and the lowest among all the counties. The next lowest is 2,900 from Northants, and all other counties have double the Derbyshire total - most in excess of 5,000.

After lunch the sun came out and so, briefly, did DiVenuto. By this time, a few hundred people were in the ground. For a while the cricket perked up, as if the real match had only now started. DiVenuto - an Australian previously registered with Sussex - was one of a clutch of players, on both sides, playing a first match for his county. For Derbyshire, Rob Bailey, Dowman and Tim Munton were also newcomers. For Leicestershire, Trevor Ward, Neil Burns, DeFreitas and Kumble were all making their entrances.

While he was at the wicket, DiVenuto changed everything. The extra-terrestrial visitor, had s(he) survived the refreshments hut, would have immediately grasped the idea of the game. DiVenuto was aided by DeFreitas who, notoriously slow to start a match, was almost visibly scraping the rust from his 34-year old limbs after the winter lay-off. In his first over after lunch the Australian cut him for four, then took further boundaries from a hoick to square leg and a cover drive. Leicestershire's management team might have permitted themselves just a frisson of concern about the value of their investment during the recess. A Derbyshire supporter, unable to believe his eyes, said: "Makes a change for us to be hammering anyone."

Though only an inch short of six feet, DiVenuto's stocky build and swaggering approach made him appear smaller. Viewed from the front, pads together, he seemed almost square. James Cagney came irresistibly to mind as the Australian took boundaries to all parts of the field. There was no

4

suggestion of elegance; he punched the ball. One smash through the covers, played waist-high, was both violent and exciting. He even took a boundary through the covers off Kumble, who had begun the first of many - Leicestershire profoundly hoped - economical and penetrating spells of leg-spin for his new county. When the batsman reached a warmly applauded 50, in 57 balls with eight boundaries, he ominously took fresh guard. It was sobering to reflect that he was probably about 15th in the pecking order of Aussies for their Test team.

Titchard succumbed half-forward to Kumble's top-spinner leaving Derbyshire at 102 for 3, and Rob Bailey came out of the pavilion to make his first contribution for Derbyshire. For a while the change put no check on DiVenuto's progress. These two batsmen represented Derbyshire's best chance of a big partnership, but it was not to be. Sadly (because life is like that) it was DiVenuto who went. He began to show signs of fallibility against Kumble, notably when Burns missed a leg-side stumping chance. There had been much discussion about the 36-year old Burns being brought back from retirement to keep to Kumble, and the Leicestershire management would have been hoping that the miss was not an omen for the season to come. When Chris Lewis came back at the grandstand end - apparently untroubled by extensive national press reports of his comments about match fixing - DiVenuto played on to his second ball. He had scored 70 from 89 balls, and it was to be the second most attractive batting in the entire match. Derbyshire were 129 for 4.

The thermometer appeared to fall by several degrees when DiVenuto departed, and it was soon clear that we had seen the best cricket of the day. In the time left, Bailey accumulated slowly, while Dominic Cork and Matthew Cassar came and went after small contributions. At stumps, Derbyshire were 227 for 6 wickets, with Bailey not out 64.

Third day

The third day (second day of play) started on time, despite a bad weather forecast. Under the stifling cloud cover it was warmer, and even the famous Derby wind had reduced in force. An eerie quiet settled over the ground. The crowd numbered a few hundred at the start.

Bailey and Krikken were already into their stride - in what turned out to be the biggest stand of the Derbyshire innings. Krikken scored much more

5

quickly, but it was Bailey's innings that attracted attention. "Was he about to settle into a productive end-of-career at Derbyshire?" would have been the thought uppermost in the minds of the Derbyshire supporters.

Bailey represents the best and the worst of English cricket. He must have posed a dilemma for the England selectors. Here was a man with a first class average of more than 41 after nearly 350 games, with 44 centuries to his name - yet he has played only four Tests. This first century for Derbyshire demonstrated why. He is an accumulator - a poor man's Atherton, without the Lancastrian's elegant cover driving or fierce hooking. His defensive strokes, inelegant prods, are almost made in two distinct phases, as if played by a robot; but - and this is the point - he usually gets bat onto ball.

As the bowler runs in to deliver the ball, Bailey's stance is a picture of extreme diffidence. There is much wandering about and tugging at clothing before he settles down. Then, legs planted apart, he stands limply in the crease, bobbing his head up and down, sliding one foot or the other along the crease, moving his bat about and - once, just before delivery - wafting it indeterminedly at shoulder height. He reminded me a little of a dog looking for somewhere to cock a leg. He must drive bowlers insane.

The Leicestershire bowling had improved upon its initial showing. Kumble wheeled away from the grandstand end, allowing no liberties, and DeFreitas was already sharper and more accurate. Both he and Lewis - when he came on - managed to get some bounce from the damp pitch. Only Ormond was disappointing - lacking accuracy and penetration - and today appearing unlikely to carry the heavier load that Leicestershire must be planning for him following the departure of Alan Mullally.

Bailey and Krikken had put on almost a hundred when the latter was leg before to DeFreitas, just after reaching his half-century. Bailey ground on with other partners, and in due course reached his century off, inevitably, a single to third man; 284 balls, with nine fours.

Before long Bailey was left with the last Derbyshire batsman as his companion, and the score past 340. It was mid-afternoon, and the only hope of a result in the match was to get Leicestershire to the crease quickly and hope to bowl them out for less than 200, force the follow-on, and bowl them out again. Still Bailey prodded on snail-like, apparently unaware of these considerations - or unable to alter his pace even after seven hours at the crease. For a while he took singles off the first ball of each over, obliging Derbyshire's last batsman to try and score from the remainder. Then he changed tack and refused several singles in a row, to 'protect' the number 11. What apparently never occurred to him was to hit out and get out, to put the game back on the rails. Nor did 12th man appear with a change of gloves, and a message to get on with it. My visitor from outer space would have been completely bemused.

There were a few murmurs among the crowd at these tactics, but the main feeling seemed to be one of relief that someone - anyone - had scored a century for Derbyshire after their batting performances in the previous season. All the same, a number of spectators had been affected by a wave of sleeping sickness. Behind me, a septuagenarian described to his companion how, at another cricket ground, his father used to buy fresh salmon sandwiches for half a crown in the 1950s. The only excitement occurred when the scoreboard operator put up the wrong total, and half a dozen people held a forum on the happening.

It was a relief when Bailey played on to Wells to end the innings. Derbyshire made 359 at 2.5 runs per over - and Bailey's innings had lasted more than seven hours.

Though the crowd remained stoical through this last, soporific passage of play, the Leicestershire players appeared to have lost heart, and to be going through the motions. The contrast was sharp when - 10 minutes after the fall of the last wicket - the Derbyshire team charged out of the pavilion, clapping and shouting, and hurling the ball about, more like a team of gladiators than cricketers. Had no-one told them that, with less than a day-and-a-half remaining and only one innings finished, the game was virtually dead?

If the plan was to give the Leicestershire batsmen the illusion that they were about to be rolled over, it worked very well for a time. Test bowler Dominic Cork, yet again with a point to make to England's selectors, charged in from the grandstand end, looking the most aggressive of all the bowlers seen so far in the match. He had Vince Wells splendidly caught by Paul Aldred, low down at point, and Darren Maddy lbw offering no stroke. When Cassar ran out Trevor Ward from cover, Leicestershire were 9 for 3, and a result did not seem so far-fetched.

Ben Smith and Aftab Habib began, slowly, to rebuild the innings, and were to put on almost 70 before another wicket fell. It was only during this passage of play, when I had had a chance to see both Derbyshire and Leicestershire batsmen at work, that the strong local affiliations of the crowd became fully apparent. In the past I had tended to go to county matches simply to watch cricket, without caring much which side was on top. A day's play is too long not to draw pleasure from performances on both sides. However, this crowd was there, as a football crowd is, to see their team win, and only secondly to see some cricket. True, Leicestershire boundaries were acknowledged, but the crowd's attention was on the Derbyshire players. For instance, Smith's elegant two runs to deep square leg was received in silence, but the accurate throw from the fielder immediately drew applause.

A different aspect of chauvinism now surfaced, as I got talking to a Derbyshire supporter who hurtled out between the ranks of parked cars and pounced on me. He wanted to know if I was a Derbyshire follower, and if I came to the ground regularly. "If anything, I follow Leicestershire," I said. "To be honest, I rarely come here. It's such an awful ground."

I felt immediately that this had not gone down well, and there was a prompt retort. "I'm not being funny," he said, "but I don't like the Leicester ground."

We never overcame the restraint caused by my tactless remark, but he gave an interesting run-down on his preferences among other grounds. He disliked Old Trafford because of "the attitude of the crowd". His favourite ground was Worcester; there was something about "drinking tea from a bone china cup".

The tea interval had now arrived. After it, both Smith and Habib fell within a few runs of each other, before play was again curtailed by bad light. Leicestershire were 100 for 5.

Fourth day

The forecast for the fourth and last day of the match was fine, but rain had fallen overnight and play was delayed by an hour. At 11.30am, half an hour after the intended starting time, I went round the ground counting spectators: 125 people in all, with possibly a few others not on show. During the course of the day this swelled to a few hundred, but it remained the smallest crowd of the three days of play - no doubt because the state of the match encouraged little hope of a result.

The loss of a further hour was a blow to Derbyshire. Their opponents - at 100 for 5 - needed 210 to avoid the follow-on, and make the game dead. There was just a chance of a result if Derbyshire could bowl them out quickly and have, say, the last two sessions to attack them again. The main stumbling blocks were likely to be the not-out batsmen who were Chris Lewis, and the young Darren Stevens.

Lewis, still chalking up column inches in newspaper reports due to his match-fixing allegations, had a customary air of impermanence. He was almost run out sauntering a single, when the fielder threw unexpectedly to his end; then he hooked high, and riskily, to the long leg boundary and, repeating the stroke when two fielders had been moved into the area, was caught at fine leg for 15. Stevens was joined by the wicket-keeper, Burns.

I had not seen Stevens play before. He was young, in English cricket terms - a day short of 24 - and had an indifferent batting average of 28 after 10 first-class games. That said, he was sometimes described in the press as a stroke-player, and 'one for the future'. Beginning the day on 10 not out, he made an immediate impression, moving his feet quickly, and playing elegantly correct forward defensive strokes to Cork and Munton. Not for long. After 10 minutes at the crease, he sent a solid-sounding straight drive to the boundary, soon followed by another through a cover region populated by three fielders, and boundaries square of the wicket on the off-side, and through mid-wicket off Cork. When he smashed a short ball one-bounce over the square leg boundary - over the head of the fielder, who slipped in going for it - the shot was greeted in silence by the crowd. This was not what Derbyshire needed at all. At 150 for 6, Leicestershire were nearly three-quarters of the way to their target.

Though the crowd failed to appreciate it, Stevens's innings was the highlight of the three days. He played with complete control and, in contrast to DiVenuto - the other batting success - little apparent aggression. His shots involved no noticeable back-lift nor a flourishing follow-through; they simply propelled the ball swiftly to the boundary with perfect timing. Apart from the hook that was nearly a six, they were all ground strokes. When he reached 50, just before lunch, it was off a mere 51 balls, with seven fours. It reminded me of the first time I saw David Gower and, as with him, I felt I was watching a future England player.

After lunch Stevens continued in this style for a time, with delightful cover drives and late cuts (for which Derbyshire stubbornly refrained from posting a third man), only disconcerted by a beamer from Trevor Smith, which sent him head over heels backwards at the crease. As the Leicestershire score approached 200 I abandoned thoughts of a follow-on and close finish, and found myself hoping for another two hours of Stevens in full flight. Fatal. Without warning, he played on to an innocuous ball from the change bowler Aldred, and was out for 78. His reluctant departure from the wicket mirrored my disappointment. In that form he must have expected - and should have got - a century.

In any first class sporting match - cricket, football, or anything else - however mundane, there are moments which make the neutral spectator's visit worthwhile. In this meaningless encounter, Stevens's innings had illuminated the afternoon, played though it was against the chill background of the Derbyshire ground, to a crowd resentful of every shot that distanced the possibility of a home victory.

Incidentally, the manner of Stevens' dismissal, which I took to be the fifth 'played on' of the match - including all three of the big scorers - said something about the variable bounce in the pitch; equally, another unusual feature - no catches to wicket-keepers or slips - indicated how little lateral movement there was in the wicket.

The game was as good as over. A mere 12 runs stood between Leicestershire and avoiding the follow-on. Soon DeFreitas sent a lofted drive over the bowler to score the two runs that took his side past the required total. It said something about the cricket that this defining moment of the whole game was received by the crowd in complete silence.

That DeFreitas went on to score 79, and Leicestershire to pass 300, was completely irrelevant - though not as irrelevant as Stubbings and Dowman scoring a total of two runs from four overs in Derbyshire's second innings, before the match was declared over by the umpires.

There was no need to consult my friend from outer space for views about the Derbyshire versus Leicestershire match. A life-long cricket fan who will watch almost anything, I nevertheless felt that if this had been my first visit to a cricket match I might never have tried again. The weather obviously played a large part in ruining the game, but there were also long stretches of cricket which defied explanation - for me, let alone a Martian. I recalled Shane Warne's comments (published in the *Cricketers' Who's Who 2000*): "Cricketers should think of themselves as entertainers for the public. They pay the money to watch cricket, then they're entitled to watch exciting cricket". I hoped profoundly that I should have better luck in my future coverage of the season's matches.

Derbyshire first innings

Batsman		Dismissal	Runs
MP Dowman		b Ormond	8
SD Stubbings	c Stevens	b DeFreitas	21
MJ DiVenuto		b Lewis	70
SP Titchard	lbw	b Kumble	8
RJ Bailey		b Wells	118
*DG Cork		b Ormond	8
ME Cassar	c Ward	b Wells	11
+KM Krikken	lbw	b DeFreitas	51
P Aldred		b Kumble	36
TA Munton		b Kumble	4
TM Smith	not out		2
Extras			22
Total	**All Out**		**359**

Bowling	O	M	R	W
Ormond	23	4	94	2
Lewis	21	4	44	1
DeFreitas	34	7	85	2
Kumble	42	13	86	3
Wells	20.3	5	40	2

Leicestershire first innings

Batsman		Dismissal	Runs
*VJ Wells	c Aldred	b Cork	0
DL Maddy	lbw	b Cork	4
TR Ward	run out		1
BF Smith	lbw	b Smith	38
A Habib	lbw	b Smith	33
DI Stevens		b Aldred	78
CC Lewis	c Smith	b Cork	15
+ND Burns	c Cork	b Cassar	37
PAJ DeFreitas	st Krikken	b Bailey	79
A Kumble	hit wicket	b Cassar	1
J Ormond	not out		1
Extras			22
Total	**All Out**		**309**

Bowling	O	M	R	W
Cork	26	8	60	3
Munton	18	2	83	0
Smith	15	2	54	2
Aldred	17	2	60	1
Cassar	9.5	5	16	2
Bailey	9	2	18	1

Derbyshire second innings

Batsman		Runs
SD Stubbings	not out	2
MP Dowman	not out	0
Extras		0
Total	**0 wickets declared**	**2**

Bowling	O	M	R	W
Maddy	2	1	2	0
Stevens	2	2	0	0

Match Drawn. Points: Derbyshire 10, Leicestershire 9

Leicestershire's cheer-leader Lewis cheering off
Darren Maddy at a one-day match (Photo: Sylvia Michael)

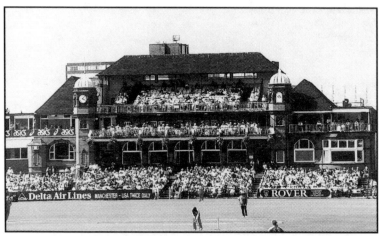

The Pavilion at Old Trafford - full for a one-day match
(Photo: Peter David Lush)

2. Lancashire versus Leicestershire
Old Trafford, 3 to 6 May

I took the Manchester Metro-Link to the Old Trafford ground, arriving at 11.30am. Leicestershire were batting, and had reached 27 for no wicket from eight overs. After the homely atmosphere of Derby, Old Trafford's Test match arena seemed enormous, like a vast, inverted spacecraft. Human figures were a rarity among the thousands of empty white seats, though the pavilion area was congested with members. An occasional, remote clunk of ball-on-bat penetrated the deep hush of the scene.

From the outset of day one in this match, it was difficult to think of anything but the cold. The forecast 'quite warm' had again been misleading; the reality was grey skies and a fierce wind, which had loose billboards flapping mournfully.

Stevens had opened with Maddy for Leicestershire, and was pushing on at a pace, and in a style, which seemed inappropriate for the bleak setting. An effortless straight drive and a fine glance for four were reprises from his Derby innings, and belonged to a different day altogether - warm sunshine, a crowd in shirtsleeves quaffing tumblers of best bitter. But when he had reached 41, out of a total of 56 for 1, he sent an easy catch to square leg off the bowling of Andrew Flintoff. Though quite clearly a catch, it was so out of character with what had gone before that Stevens - as he had in his Derby dismissal - hesitated at the crease before departing. "Did I do that?" he appeared to be thinking. "Can I stop doing that, and build an innings?"

" 'E didn't want to go," said a spectator, seeing Stevens tarry. "It weren't in the script". The voice came from one of half-a-dozen old codgers sitting in a group four rows behind me, all in their 60s or 70s, and all wearing flat caps. They might have been paid to appear there as local colour by the Lancashire Tourist Board. The men were keeping the cold at bay with an unending stream of chatter. Some of this concerned cricket, and some of it 'life' in general. 'Money' was a recurring theme.

"All the die 'ards are 'ere, aren't they. There's not many paid today."

"We don't want any black market in pensioners' tickets, Arthur."

"I don't know what they charge for top balcony."

"Prices were way down for three months, and then they go back up again."

"15 million - it's ridiculous!"

"They've ruined every pub in the area."

After Stevens went, Leicestershire batted with a circumspection more suited to the temperature. Lunch found them at 104 for 4, with no-one else having taken on the accurate Lancashire bowling. It was hard to concentrate on the cricket. I was in a couple of sweaters, but had never felt so cold at a match. The 1,500-strong Lancashire crowd, inured to the conditions, sat on stoically. Apparently the day before had been fine and this, together with the optimistic forecast, had misled many spectators into turning up under-dressed. Several men were in shirt-sleeves, and one ruddy-faced chap in a blazer and straw hat seemed to have consulted the forecast for a different country altogether. Even so, the intensity of cold dragged some comments on the conditions out of a few of the more wimpish spectators. I noticed, looking round the ground, that various people were - like myself - positioned at the back of the stand jumping up and down and flapping their arms, as if we were all part of a gigantic performance of *Grease*, or some other musical production.

As lunch approached, the small group behind me got louder. Despite their age, they probably thought of themselves as 'the lads'; indeed had once been 'the lads'. A similar group of thirty year olds would have been labelled 'lager louts', but the flasks of the ancients contained tea rather than alcohol, and their high spirits were fuelled by nothing more than cheese sandwiches and sausage rolls. The ring-leader brought the morning to a close with an impassioned speech - punctuated by cries of "give over" from his companions - against 'technology', starting with mobile phones and ending up by savaging the motor car.

The interval came, and I set off round the ground to find something to eat and drink. This was more difficult than anticipated. A complete circuit of Old Trafford unearthed only a hot dog stand (where you could get a plastic cup of what appeared to be dishwater for £1) and an ice-cream van. Later, I actually saw a man sucking an iced lolly - the equivalent of Captain Scott including portions of baked Alaska in his provisions for the Antarctic.

A steward advised that there was a place where food could be obtained. An unmarked door led into a corridor, thence to a large open space with a bar and a dozen large tables, and a buffet offering meat or fish, with vegetables. Matronly ladies in black skirts and white blouses presided over a congregation of white-haired gentlemen munching their way through this

14

traditional fare. It reminded me of the catering arrangements for a senior citizens tour. Not a mobile phone in sight.

After Derby, and now this, I could already feel myself turning into a cricket catering bore. Why were facilities for non-members so poor at the county grounds? It is ridiculous that a big club like Lancashire did not seem to make available a range of sandwiches and a decent cup of coffee, and does not even signpost the main food source at the ground. The attitude is very clear: here county cricket is an insiders' club for members and regulars, and if you are not one of these you can fend for yourself. Yet visitors to a cricket match tend to remain all day, need refreshment during their stay, and are more likely to become regulars if the management provides decent facilities. I could not imagine younger spectators sitting through the traditional catering - and indeed none had been there. Clubs seem to be doing their best to cut off the supply of their future members.

Following the lunch interval, Leicestershire struggled on in unpromising conditions, with the ball moving about under the overcast sky. No individual batsman dominated, but Vince Wells - Leicestershire's new captain - made the innings's top score with a half-century. The man of the day was a bowler. Peter Martin's big, square-looking figure charged in to the wicket with whole-hearted enthusiasm for long spells of the play, on a day when running about was preferable to standing still at long leg. At the beginning of each over the umpire was loaded with three Martin sweaters, and the bowler's serial efforts to put these back on again as he walked down to the boundary were an entertainment in itself. By close of play Martin had 30 overs and six wickets under his belt. The wickets were due reward for obliging batsmen to play at most of his deliveries.

The spectators were more objective than those at the Derby ground. They supported Lancashire all right - of that there was no doubt - but equally, they offered warm applause for any good piece of cricket from either side. Another pleasing advance on Derby was the style of the announcements, which were perky and definitely not pompous - a minor detail, but the announcer exercises a cumulative influence on the spirits of the crowd.

An hour from the close Leicestershire lost their ninth wicket to a slip catch by Michael Atherton. Apart from a brief spell in the covers, Atherton had been standing in the slips for most of the day, inactive except when he plunged to earth to avoid being beheaded by a ball which went for four wides. When DeFreitas deflected a ball from Martin low to first slip,

Atherton swooped undemonstrably to pick it up two-handed. He is a professional.

This left Leicestershire at 218 for 9, and it looked as if Lancashire would have to end the day with an hour's batting. James Ormond and Anil Kumble, the last-wicket pair, had other ideas. With his six feet three inches and nearly 15 stone, it was no surprise to see Ormond make some powerful blows; but what took the eye - in between some playing and missing - was the quality of his stroke-play. He struck several fours and a six, and an imposing force through the covers off the back foot brought up his team's 250. As the afternoon wore on John Crawley probably kept on Martin and Chris Schofield, both into long spells, for too long.

I had taken up yet another position in the stands, this time behind the bowler's arm - the most populated part of the otherwise untenanted public seating, where bodies had accumulated as though washed up and stranded by an outgoing tide. During this last-wicket stand I began at last to feel that I was adapting, after a long lay-off, to the rhythm needed for watching cricket: a patient, observant, solitary approach, like that of a fisherman awaiting a catch on the river bank. The evening light slowly failed, and a pallid sun drifted behind the clouds over the arena. One by one the old men rose from their seats and departed. A plastic bag pirouetted in the breeze, and a magpie descended onto the back of a seat in front of me, hopping along the row in search of food. The hush over the ground intensified, broken by an occasional cry from the fielders, and the clanking of trams pulling out of the Metro-Link station. Despite the chill, I felt at home, and found myself greatly looking forward to the summer's cricket.

Second Day

Next morning, as so often happens after a stand the night before, the last wicket fell immediately. Atherton again took the catch, off Martin, and the fielders turned in unison towards the pavilion, body language declaring "that's got that bit of nonsense over with". Leicestershire were all out for 265, with Martin returning superb figures of 7 for 67.

The Lancashire innings did not start well. In the second over, Atherton smashed a short, wide delivery from Lewis to point, where Kumble took a fierce catch. Soon after this, Ward held an even better one low down at second slip to dismiss Crawley off Ormond. Lancashire were 15 for 2, with their two best-known batsmen back in the pavilion.

But this Lancashire batting order was the most impressive among all the counties. It had five batsmen in the 'top 30' of players currently featuring in the championship, and a long tail, plus the joker card of Andrew Flintoff - who had come in to bat in the unaccustomed position of first-wicket-down. At Crawley's departure he was joined by Saurav Ganguly, the Indian batsman whom Lancashire had taken as their overseas player for the season. The Lancashire members left the Indian in no doubt that they were pleased to have him, greeting his appearance with an unusually warm burst of applause.

Flintoff has one of the most recognisable profiles in English cricket. He is six feet four inches high, but it is his torso which takes the eye. Seen from a distance it seems to belong to a portly player nearing the end of his career, rather than a 22-year-old bristling with muscle (sometimes augmented, it is often said, with an indiscreet helping of fat). It was soon apparent that this mountain of flesh was being differently disposed at the wicket. The point made about Flintoff's innings by all the papers on the following day was his new stance, relaxed and upright in place of his old crouch, and presumed to be the handiwork of Lancashire's new Australian coach, Bobby Simpson. There were also comments about the focused and 'gentle' Flintoff supplanting the player who had made violent but brief appearances at the wicket in previous seasons.

These were over stated, since Flintoff's enormous power was frequently exercised in the innings; what we did see was better technical organisation in his new role at first-wicket-down, and greater selectivity in shot-making. Even his defensive play was engaging to watch, because Flintoff has a way of freezing for a couple of seconds after a stroke, transforming himself into a massive, granite statue - a Colossus of Rhodes.

After flicking a four off his legs, Flintoff sent a second boundary crashing through the slips area with enough force to take off the fielders' finger-tips. The axiom "if you're going to slash, slash hard" could have been invented by him. He followed this with two straight drives - precursors of what was probably his most productive stroke. When he smashed another delivery through the covers off the back foot, none of the fielders moved for a second, and the whereabouts of the ball was made known to spectators only by Leicestershire players turning their heads towards the boundary.

Meanwhile Ganguly was playing himself in very carefully - for the season, one felt, and not just for this innings. After an hour and 40 minutes of play Flintoff had scored 36; there were 6 extras, and the rest had 9 between them.

As soon as the Indian leg-spinner Kumble entered the attack, Ganguly came into his own and immediately went down the wicket to advise Flintoff how to play him. It was Ganguly who reached out expansively to send Kumble sweetly through the covers, then delightfully flicked him for four to the long leg area. The contrast between Flintoff's power and Ganguly's wristy, typically Indian play made them most pleasing partners for the Lancashire crowd.

Lunch took place at 75 for 2, with Flintoff on 45. Such early exchanges often determine the course of a match, and Leicestershire were unlucky in the weather, for the heavy cloud which covered their entire innings had given way to clear skies, giving the bowlers less movement in the air. Nevertheless there were moments when the game might have changed direction. Flintoff had played and missed several times, and once was nearly caught by Lewis, diving full-length to a drive at mid-on. Had Leicestershire posted a third slip Flintoff would have been snapped up there off one of his furious slashes.

After lunch Ganguly, to general regret, was caught at the wicket off Lewis for 30. There was no respite for Leicestershire, because Neil Fairbrother now joined Flintoff in a partnership which was to last until the tea interval. The contrast in appearance between the two men was striking, with a difference of eight inches between them vertically (and probably horizontally as well). That was not the only contrast. Fairbrother's knack of nurdling short singles behind the wicket, particularly to leg, must have been instructive for Flintoff, who rarely scored behind unless by accident.

Examples of these 'accidents' were not rare. Just after reaching his half-century, Flintoff should have been caught by Kumble, running in from third man, off a swirling mis-stroke which came to ground between point and third man boundary. It almost happened again later on, off a mis-timed hook, with Ormond the fielder running in from the same position. These blemishes apart, there were some memorable strokes: a four through extra cover from no more than a push, another from crashing Wells back over his head, and another boundary (almost a six) to square leg off Wells to take him to his century. Just before tea a similar stroke did go for six. The tea-time score of

233 for 3, with Flintoff on 119 and Fairbrother already - ominously - on 60, did not bode well for Leicestershire.

The tea-time announcements of scores from other grounds brought a result which drew delighted exclamations from the crowd. Durham had beaten Surrey, the county champions, by an innings and 231 runs in a low-scoring match, bowling out Surrey for 85 in their second innings. The result set the newly introduced two-division County Championship alive, after the delays caused by bad weather.

Off the first ball after tea, Flintoff was caught by Lewis at mid-on off DeFreitas, going for a big hit. He went off sheepishly, no doubt preparing excuses for Bobby Simpson, while DeFreitas celebrated unusually by giving Lewis a piggy-back. But there was no let-up for Leicestershire. Both Graham Lloyd and Warren Hegg contributed quick runs, while Fairbrother continued sedately to his 41st first-class century. The Leicestershire bowlers and fielders did not throw in the towel - far from it - but the evening sunshine brought a sense of resignation, together with a continuous chuntering sound among them as they sought to keep their spirits up. Somewhat strangely, Lewis could be overheard discussing a financial deal with one of his colleagues. At stumps Lancashire were 342 for 5, and the match was almost settled.

Third day

Any hopes that Leicestershire may have retained were quickly dispelled on the third morning by Chris Schofield, coming in after the immediate dismissal of Hegg, and wearing an elongated sweater that could almost have served as a dressing-gown. He got off the mark with a single wide of cover, pulled Ormond violently for four, and sent a ball from Lewis through the covers with a very solid-sounding bat. Schofield was not so much as a fidgeter as a long distance runner. Between balls he would hop back about 10 yards from the crease, or run about in small circles, or indulge in extensive gardening half-way down the pitch. He was never still during the bowler's run-in.

Thirty runs were added in the first half-hour of the day and, by the time Fairbrother was caught at the wicket for 138, the Lancashire score had raced past the 400 mark. Schofield reached his highest first-class score (39) with a slash over point, and then his first 50 with a single pushed off Kumble.

Lunch arrived with Lancashire 451 for 7. Schofield was eventually last out for 66 in comical fashion, attempting a reverse sweep off Kumble, the ball hitting the back of his bat and rolling onto the stumps. Lancashire's total was formidable: 488, with a day-and-a-half to bowl Leicestershire out again.

None of the bowlers' figures were flattering, but Ormond had impressed by bowling 34 overs and taking four wickets; he had most of the batsmen in trouble at some stage. He came to the wicket fairly relaxed, off a longish run, before using powerful shoulders to release the ball at a decidedly sharp pace. Prior to this season his 136 wickets at an average of 24.2 - in only a couple of seasons - had been an impressive return. The England selectors were likely to be watching him closely.

With a first-innings deficit of more than 200 Leicestershire can have held few hopes of avoiding defeat, and their chances were not improved when Stevens was out in exactly the same manner as in the first innings - caught at square leg off Glen Chapple by Graham Lloyd, who seconds before had been deep in conversation with the umpire. Shortly after this, Lloyd also snapped up Ward, hooking in ungainly fashion at the same bowler.

Chapple's third wicket owed everything to Flintoff, and was alone worth the price of admission. Ben Smith, in full flow, flashed at the ball, which flew hard and low wide of second slip, where Flintoff somehow got his vast frame down to ground level and snatched up the ball.

I went to stretch my legs and watch the game from the fence near the parking area. Leaning against the railings was one of the younger Lancashire members - not a day over 55 - bearded, unusually scruffy (for a member) in a donkey jacket and track suit trousers. He impressed immediately with his knowledge of the game and balanced views: keenly observant (had Stevens played early at Chapple's slower ball?); well informed about details (who was doing well in the Lancashire second team, Fairbrother's age - which I had guessed at, wrongly); objective in his assessments ("no point in keep switching personnel around when you have reliable bowlers already"); generous about the players ("a really friendly bunch"); and self-deprecatory ("I can't take to this new scoreboard - see how stuck in my ways I am"). It was agreeable talking to him, and left a very favourable impression of the regular cricket-watcher.

The Lancashire members as a whole were in rare good humour in the evening sunlight, as it became clear that their team were marking up an early, impressive win in the new championship. They had laughed at

Schofield's bizarre dismissal; they chortled when a stroke rebounded off the massive, motionless figure of Flintoff at forward short leg; and they almost fell off their chairs when the announcer's mobile phone bleeped in mid-announcement, and was magnified all around the ground.

One of the pleasures of the final session was a second look at the bowling of Schofield, who was given a long spell after getting Maddy caught at slip, leaving Leicestershire at 79 for 4. He had an easy approach off a very short run - in essence, only three paces - and slung the ball down at a pretty quick (almost Underwood-ish) pace. Despite the brisk delivery, he was clearly spinning the ball quite a bit, and this on early-season pitches.

There was also a nice moment from the other young Lancashire bowler. Michael Smethurst was a 23-year-old medium-pacer, slightly reminiscent in built of Brian Statham, playing only his fifth match for Lancashire's first team. He had had a miserable first innings, going for 50 runs without reward in 10 overs, and clearly nervous, he began his spell in the second innings in similar vein. To make matters worse a very effective bouncer - much faster than his customary medium fast pace - almost invariably caused him to over-step, and be called for a no-ball. One could feel the frustration of a young player trying to establish himself in the first team, and aware that there may not be too many chances to do so. Crawley persevered with him, and at length Habib pulled a delivery to mid-on. Smethurst literally danced for joy, and the Lancashire players rushed to congratulate him. As things turned out, he was to take a lot more wickets for Lancashire during the season.

By the time Lewis was out, again caught hooking, the match was over. The next morning Schofield quickly finished off the tail, ending with 4 for 82. Only the Leicestershire captain, Wells - with 46 - offered any prolonged resistance. Lancashire had a substantial victory.

Leicestershire first innings

DL Maddy		b Chapple	6
DI Stevens	c Schofield	b Flintoff	41
TR Ward		b Martin	39
BF Smith	c Hegg	b Flintoff	4
A Habib	lbw	b Martin	4
*VJ Wells	c Hegg	b Martin	56
CC Lewis	lbw	b Martin	24
+ND Burns	c Hegg	b Martin	6
PAJ DeFreitas	c Atherton	b Martin	1
A Kumble	c Atherton	b Martin	15
J Ormond	not out		30
Extras			39
Total	All Out		**265**

Bowling	O	M	R	W
Martin	31.5	9	67	7
Chapple	16	4	39	1
Flintoff	18	7	31	2
Smethurst	10	1	50	0
Ganguly	7	2	24	0
Schofield	22	6	47	0

Lancashire first innings

Batsman		Dismissal	Runs
MA Atherton	c Kumble	b Lewis	1
*JP Crawley	c Ward	b Ormond	1
A Flintoff	c Lewis	b DeFreitas	119
SC Ganguly	c Burns	b Lewis	30
NH Fairbrother	c Burns	b DeFreitas	138
GD Lloyd	c Burns	b Ormond	24
+WK Hegg		b Kumble	29
CP Schofield		b Kumble	66
G Chapple	c Maddy	b Ormond	25
PJ Martin	c Burns	b Ormond	16
MP Smethurst	not out		0
Extras			39
Total	All Out		**488**

Bowling	O	M	R	W
Ormond	34	6	122	4
Lewis	20	0	108	2
DeFreitas	34	13	84	2
Kumble	36.1	11	93	2
Wells	17	3	59	0
Maddy	2	0	9	0

Leicestershire second innings

Batsman		Dismissal	Runs
DL Maddy	c Ganguly	b Schofield	18
DI Stevens	c Lloyd	b Chapple	7
TR Ward	c Lloyd	b Chapple	4
BF Smith	c Flintoff	b Chapple	19
A Habib	c Martin	b Smethurst	37
*VJ Wells	c Ganguly	b Schofield	45
CC Lewis	c Schofield	b Flintoff	5
+ND Burns	st Hegg	b Schofield	28
PAJ DeFreitas		b Martin	13
A Kumble		b Schofield	0
J Ormond	not out		0
Extras			22
Total	All Out		**198**

Bowling	O	M	R	W
Martin	26	9	44	1
Chapple	12	1	43	3
Schofield	27.1	6	82	4
Smethurst	6	2	13	1
Flintoff	8	4	8	1

Lancashire won by an innings and 25 runs. Points: Lancashire 20, Leicestershire 4

3. Leicestershire versus Somerset
Grace Road, 11 to 14 May

At the start of Leicestershire's first home match of the season I set off for the ground where I expected to be watching a good deal of cricket during the coming year. It was just after 11am and, looking for the entrance, I walked up and down Grace Road - the name by which the county ground is always known. The street was deserted. At Old Trafford I had complained that they did not advertise the catering facilities. At Grace Road they do not advertise the ground. There were no signs at all indicating the existence of a large cricket ground alongside the stretch of red-brick suburban road. I searched for at least 10 minutes until, eventually, an old lady appeared, shuffling down the unoccupied street - the only survivor, it seemed, of a nuclear attack on Leicester. In answer to my enquiry she directed me down a three-feet wide dirt track between wooden fences. At the end of it was a county cricket ground.

"Is this the main gate to the Leicestershire ground?" I asked the white-coated attendant, expecting a denial.

"That's right."

"There are no signs to it."

"I know there aren't."

Of course, it is hardly likely that someone who has taken the trouble to find Grace Road will abandon their search for the ground and go away, but the lack of signing again says something about the ingrown clubbiness of county cricket. If you are a member you will know where the ground is; and if you are not a member... well, you should be.

That said, the ground itself made an immediately favourable impression. It is an attractive, homely and varied place, surrounded by trees on much of its perimeter, well maintained, with any number of different seating options and - please note, Derby and Old Trafford - catering options.

Membership here offers a very good deal, with a basic subscription of £43 - cheaper than any county in either division, with the exception of Glamorgan. And, by courtesy of a new arrangement, this price also secures free entrance to the grounds at Derby, Nottingham and Northampton. That the cost of membership is crucial became clear the next day, when I talked to a pensioner who had changed to Leicestershire after a life-long allegiance to

Northamptonshire cricket. Why the change? "The price," he said simply. "And the facilities here are better."

Somerset were batting, and DeFreitas and Ormond pounding in to bowl. Both sides were short of bowlers because of injuries. Leicestershire had lost Wells and Lewis. (After playing two matches consecutively, Lewis was missing for a third.) Somerset, one felt, had the worst of it, losing their opening pair, Andy Caddick and Matthew Bulbeck. Caddick was on the ground, but suffering from a blistered toe which he felt should be rested - an early instance of the new England central test match contracts affecting counties.

The pitch was slow. Neither Ormond nor DeFreitas were getting any bounce, though even at this early stage the occasional ball kept low. Kumble was on early, but also got little change from the surface. "Don't seem to be 'aving much trouble 'gainst Kumble, do they?" observed a spectator. Lunch was taken at 76 for 2 - a classic luncheon score - with Marcus Trescothick on 37.

I watched the early post-lunch play from the refreshment room, where a series of big picture windows give a superb view of the play. The place has its regular inhabitants, some of whom never seem to shift out of it.

"Just right, 'ere," said one elderly chap. "Comfortable seat, nice and warm, good view."

" 'Tis a good view an' all," said his companion.

For some of the regulars the refreshment room was a gentleman's club, with only remotely cricketing connections. As I ate a sandwich, watching the opening overs after lunch, my two neighbours talked over all manner of things: what they had for breakfast; a friend who had just "bought" a Filipino wife; another friend who claimed he had bedded the wife and daughter of the same family, and now had designs on his Member of Parliament. Cricket was not mentioned.

Soon after lunch the substitute Leicestershire captain, Ben Smith, switched round Ormond and DeFreitas, a move which brought an immediate change in the game. Ormond trapped Peter Bowler leg before; then, beating beat Burns for pace, had him looping a catch off the glove to the Leicestershire wicket-keeper. Immediately the dangerous stroke-player, Rob Turner, was out to Ormond's next ball, playing no stroke. (Actually, "no stroke" is too positive a description for the reaction from Turner, who seemed merely to be admiring his bat; "no 'no stroke'" would be more accurate.) Suddenly, Somerset were 88 for 5, and Ormond had taken three wickets.

Before too long both Keith Parsons and Graham Rose had also fallen, leaving Somerset apparently down and out at 138 for 7. I was down by the pavilion when Parsons walked back there. The expression of utter dejection on his face said something about county players' commitment - often questioned in the popular press.

This area, in front of the pavilion and restaurant and behind the sightscreen, is an extremely agreeable one at the Grace Road ground. A stretch of paving runs along it - on which the cricketers, in their studs, sound like horses - and members are crammed into nooks and crannies of seating all around, chattering away and fetching drinks from the bar. The Leicestershire spectators are a much more mixed bunch than I had observed at Derby or Old Trafford, with plenty of husband-and-wife and father-and-son combinations, quite a few women, and (most encouraging of all) a lot of younger people. There is a constant hum of conversation. Players, coming and going from the pavilion, are an integral part of the scene. Every time one shows up small boys materialise from nowhere to press for autographs, and it is rare for a player to decline. In mid-afternoon Andy Caddick was furiously busy, juggling 12th-man duties with good-natured signing, putting the lie to a concerted two-year press campaign presenting him as a disagreeable loner.

There was always a knot of people standing round the entrance to the bar, and it was here that I discovered the owner of the piercing voice heard blasting across the Derbyshire ground two weeks earlier. Lewis was a middle-aged West Indian - short, round, very smartly dressed - who had taken up a permanent position at the bar door and an unofficial role as Leicestershire cheerleader. Any piece of play favourable to Leicestershire had him running around behind the sightscreen with arms held out horizontally - like a small propeller plane trying to take off - bawling out in a voice which carried to all corners of the ground. The content was hard to decipher, but an occasional phrase came through clearly. ("Everybody happy?" "This is cricket." "Wicket to wicket, bowler".) He was assiduous about keeping the umpires up to the mark. ("Use them fingers, umpire".) Often in conversation with the players' wives and other camp-followers he would, when amused, involuntarily release a series of shrieks at short intervals; heard from the other side of the pitch, these suggested that a hyena had, by some improbable mischance, gained entrance to the ground.

Not everyone approved of Lewis's antics, and there was the occasional cry of "Shut up" from older members, but on balance he was an asset and a focus for Leicestershire supporters. Watching cricket seemed to be his full-time occupation; I overheard him say to one of the women "I be still here when I die".

The optimism that had spread tangibly among Leicestershire supporters when Somerset were 138 for 7 began to dissipate as Trescothick was joined by a young player, Ian Blackwell, and a stand developed. After 85 overs the two had taken the score to 200 for 7.

"A bit of a nuisance, these blokes, aren't they?" said a member to his neighbour.

The Somerset point of view was heard more rarely, naturally enough, but one got a sense of their commitment from a man in a blazer standing at the entrance to the pavilion, clearly related to the Somerset team in some official capacity. "Go on," he urged quietly to himself, as Trescothick turned the ball to third man. "*Go* on. Make it three. Go on."

Go on they did. Trescothick had played with absolute certainty from the start of the day, and anchored the Somerset innings, not at all fazed by wickets falling at the other end. He was a player often mentioned in despatches, and had been on the recent England A tour to Bangladesh and New Zealand. Later in the season he was to make an impressive debut for the full England one-day team. He scored slowly, but the innings was decorated with lovely strokes all round the wicket - drives through cover and straight, hooks, sweeps, clever deflections through the slips, and one savage pull to the mid-wicket boundary. Blackwell was an ideal partner, belying his 'number 11' status on the scorecard by scoring at the fastest rate of the day. "If he's a number 11, I can bat as well," said a spectator.

The Trescothick-Blackwell partnership endured through tea, and on towards the end of the day. Blackwell was through the 40s in no time, with a cover drive followed by a six to square leg. At 5.30pm, Trescothick reached the bigger milestone with a single. They were both out just before the close to Kumble, taking home wickets at last, and the Somerset innings finished on 262.

Second day

On day two, Leicestershire's reply began disastrously. Though deprived of both Caddick and Bulbeck, Somerset fielded an impressive pair of opening bowlers. Graham Rose had been a Somerset all-rounder since 1987, but it was still a surprise to learn that he had more than 570 first-class wickets to his name. Big and strong, with a James Ormond type of frame, he powered in from the Bennett end to show a lot of pace. His partner, Jamie Grove, was almost unknown, with a mere eight first-class matches and 14 wickets behind him. He generated almost as much speed from a slender frame and whippy action. They had very different ways of running up to the wicket, with Grove sprinting all out, and Rose taking a lot of much shorter steps, as if running up a slope.

The trouble started when Maddy was bowled by Grove playing no stroke - as he had (or rather, had not) at Derby. It was 20 for 1. Within short order, Stevens and Ward were leg before to Rose, and Smith was caught in the slips, to chortles of joy from the fielders. Leicestershire were 34 for 4 before midday, with their last two batsmen at the wicket.

This pair could not have been more different, in style or appearance. Most cricket followers might think of Aftab Habib as the player who had frozen when picked for England against New Zealand the previous season, and been immediately dropped. Notwithstanding this setback, he had a first class average of 43.6, which put him right up among the best English players. He is a stocky figure, neat and composed at the wicket.

John Dakin is a different kettle of fish. He made his debut for Leicestershire in 1993, but has never really established himself in the side, playing only 33 matches in the past seven years. That said, he is a more than handy all-rounder: a useful change bowler, and a batsman with an average of nearly 30 and four centuries to his name. Dakin is an unmistakable figure on a cricket pitch, six feet four inches high, and with a weight described in the *Cricketers' Who's Who* (perhaps a trifle economically) as 16 stone, much of it distributed above the waist in imposing shoulders and diaphragm, giving him a top-heavy look; once, leaning backwards, he appeared almost to topple over as the weight of this upper half obeyed Newton's law of gravity. From a distance he reminded me of Bob Hope.

Slowly, this ill-matched combination began rebuilding the innings. Habib has a natural tendency to play himself in before showing aggression. Dakin -

according to one spectator - was more likely to shoot from the hip straight away. This time he forced himself to be more circumspect. It was a nervous passage of play, and spectators were anxious or resigned, according to temperament. At the door of the bar, Lewis was like a cat on hot bricks, prowling his territory and responding unfathomably to Somerset appeals.

"Aun-tie-bedit," to a rejected appeal from Parsons.

"Wan-you-ged-id," to one from Trescothick.

"Dis-de-dat-cricket-ade-wicket," triumphantly as Habib cut Parsons to the boundary for four.

There is no real explanation for the curious cricket phenomenon when a single player appears supremely confident at the wicket while his team-mates all struggle? It had happened the day before with Trescothick, and today Habib was completely composed from the start. He began by pushing comfortable twos and threes through the field, before unleashing two cover boundaries and a straight drive for four in a single over from Parsons. His method was based upon neat and assured defence; once established, he blossomed into elegant strokes to all parts - rarely violent, always playing within himself. His cover and straight driving was without blemish, but added to this were delightful deflections to the third man and long leg boundaries. Best of all were strokes off his legs to the mid-wicket area, which at one point led to five men being posted in the leg-side field - still punctured periodically by Habib's accuracy.

For an hour or so, Habib was the dominant partner. At lunch, taken at 97 for 4, he had 41 to Dakin's 18. Afterwards, with the spinners on, Dakin slashed at Blackwell and missed, then edged the following ball through the slips. Ominously for Somerset, this was almost the end of his uncertainty. In the next over Dakin advanced yards from his crease and struck Blackwell through mid-on, then did it again straight. As his innings caught fire, it became clear that John Dakin liked driving. His height and enormous reach, and willingness to come down the pitch (which Habib did rarely) gave him a big advantage, and he began to score freely in the 'V' between cover and mid-wicket.

With both batsmen well set, Somerset's attack was really put to the test. Rose came back, at 125 for 4, but did not stem the flow. A cover drive from Habib brought up the 100 partnership, and shortly afterwards Dakin reached his half-century with three through the same area. The crowd were basking in sunlight now, coats off, white hats on, beers in hand, appreciative but still watchful. When Habib fenced at Grove in mid-afternoon, with a rare false shot, Lewis's reproach immediately floated across the ground: "Don' do any fishin'."

Habib redeemed himself with a rare excursion down the wicket to hit Pierson past mid-wicket.

"Yeeeeeah! Yeeeeeah! Dis is cricket. Dis is cricket."

The Somerset fielders kept their spirits up, but the milestones began to pass more quickly: the 150 partnership and, just before tea Leicestershire's 200. Habib was 92, and Dakin 65. From a position of 34 for 4 it seemed, for Leicestershire supporters, too good to be true. "Everybody happy? I'm happy."

After tea Habib wasted no time in going to his ninth first-class century, with a straight drive off Parsons, followed by a cover drive. I had for the first time gone up into the small stand high above the sightscreen at the pavilion end, which afforded a wonderful view behind the bowler's arm. The height of this small seating area made it into a sort of eyrie, detached from the rest of the ground. The weather was closing in, and against a backdrop of a glowering sky, Dakin and Habib put the Somerset attack to the sword. There were no false strokes now. You felt they could do no wrong.

Habib pulled Blackwell to the mid-wicket boundary to bring up the 200 partnership - how often do you see one of those in county cricket - but it was John Dakin who became the more flamboyant partner. To tired Somerset fielders, who might (at 34 for 4) have thought they had the match won, he must have looked a colossus, striding down the wicket to smash them back to the far corners of the ground. He hit Blackwell for a straight six, then in the same over crashed a boundary through mid-off to bring up his century. For the second time since tea, he and Habib embraced warmly mid-pitch. They had reached their milestones at a remarkably similar rate, with Dakin taking 222 balls against Habib's 214 and hitting the same number of fours (14), plus his six.

Somerset's spirit was at last beginning to flag. The long, hot day in the field, thwarted ambition, the left-hand, right-hand partnership, and the batsmen's utter dominance were taking their toll. Leicestershire had taken the total to 275, and the partnership to 241, when the umpires conferred about the light and the batsmen, surprisingly, came off. They returned to the pavilion to applause which recognised that something special had happened.

I noticed that neither Habib nor Dakin were smiling; there was still a job to be done.

The public address system announced that they had beaten the previous-highest partnership against Somerset, set by Roger Tolchard and A. N. Other. "I liked old Roger Tolchard," said a middle-aged lady by the sight screen.

Excited, like everyone else, I talked to a chap of Indian origin, who said he had supported Leicestershire for 17 seasons. "I would just love to see that championship pennant hanging up there again," he said. Watching them was like a drug. "I have even missed family occasions that I ought to have gone to. I've done it." Given the strength of Indian family ties, this was some admission.

Amid the euphoria, I felt a nagging worry that the batsmen had chosen to go off in light that was indifferent, but not really bad. Another hour's batting in that utterly dominant vein might make all the difference in a tight match, on a good pitch. Then I thought: hell, it was churlish to complain. It had been a marvellous day.

Third day

Next morning, the pair went on for a while in a quieter vein, unable - not surprisingly - to reproduce the pyrotechnics of the previous evening. All the same, when Dakin was very well caught low down at mid-on by Cox, they had taken the score to 309, and the partnership to 275 - the third highest ever for Leicestershire's fifth wicket. Habib continued, unperturbed, to build his innings, while a variety of partners lost their wickets at the other end. When Leicestershire were all out after lunch for 387, Habib was still there with 172 off 380 balls, including 21 fours.

Somerset began their reply at 2.50pm. They were 125 runs behind the Leicestershire total, with a day-and-a-half to play. Victory seemed beyond them, so it was a question of whether they could bat until mid-afternoon the following day, scoring enough runs to prevent their opponents from passing the aggregate total in a - potentially - brief fourth innings. It was going to be a hard grind. Leicestershire would want at least three or four wickets during the afternoon and evening.

They did not come. Trescothick began as he had left off in the first innings, this time accompanied by Cox, playing very positively. The pitch looked as slow as ever, and even flatter. The pair took the score to 49 by tea, and then ground on into the evening. Leicestershire tried all their bowlers. DeFreitas looked weary, and one could imagine him thinking - have I got to bowl on this shirt front all season? Spectators were tense. Lewis, wearing a Mexican sombrero, was otherwise undemonstrative. A pensioner lamented at length the lack of draught Bass in the pavilion bar. A lurcher dog, bereft of political correctness, barked furiously at a man passing in a wheelchair.

At last, with the score at 66, Cox was caught at the wicket off Kumble. The Indian leg-spinner was bowling in relatively short spells, mostly from the Bennett end, occasionally switching round. It was becoming clear already that Leicestershire's fortunes in this match - perhaps all season - would rest in large part upon his shoulders. That was fine by me, because watching him bowl was a pleasure.

Kumble looks a class performer even when standing about in the outfield. His profile is unmistakably South Indian - handsome, aquiline, dark glossy hair brushed back. From a distance he looks taller than his six feet one inch suggests, perhaps because his legs seem to reach up to his armpits. Running in to bowl, he first holds the ball up in his left hand, showing it to the batsman like a conjuror about to indulge in some sleight-of-hand; then bounds in, transferring it to his right, leaps high, and hurls the ball down - quite quickly for a spinner. There is a vibrant, electric feel about the whole process. No-one would need to be told that here is a world-class bowler at work, but if need be, the figures tell the story: 239 Test wickets by the age of 30, and only the second bowler to take 10 wickets in a Test match innings - lucky Leicestershire. What may he achieve during the summer, as the wickets dry out and become harder?

When Trescothick was on 43, Kumble had him extremely well caught, low down at leg slip, by Maddy. Leicestershire would have been heartily glad to see the back of him. But that was the last success of the day. Holloway appeared to have been caught at forward short leg, but was not given, and he and Bowler played out the day, leaving Leicestershire well short of requirements.

All that remained was to marvel at some of the fielders' antics as they exercised between overs. At one point Ormond seemed to have fallen face down in despair at the edge of the track, callously ignored by his team-mates. Stranger still, second slip was lying on his back in a posture entirely new to the training manual, showing an expanse of bottom, surmounted by legs trembling in the air. It looked as if the county had contracted a giant jelly fish to field in the slip area.

Towards the end of the day, Kumble bowled a full toss. Peter Bowler was so surprised that he did not get it off the square.

Fourth day

At the beginning of the last day, the odds seemed on a draw - with a Leicestershire victory possible, and a Somerset victory only remotely possible. The first few overs from DeFreitas brightened his side's prospects. Holloway was caught behind. Then Burns played on, while trying to remove his bat from the line of fire. Somerset 130 for 4.

This was a success - the only one for some while - for the substitute captain Ben Smith, who had opened with his fast bowlers rather than Kumble. Bowler was batting fluently, looking just the man to score a tenacious hundred to save the game, and he was joined by Rob Turner, who had a reputation for quick scoring. They saw off the fast bowlers, and survived a number of lbw appeals from Kumble. Finally one was given, as Turner missed a full-length ball. Somerset 170 for 5, 45 runs ahead.

Parsons proved a more than adequate replacement. He and Bowler took play through the lunch interval and into mid-afternoon. The score passed 200 - 75 ahead. Parsons was dropped at slip, off Dakin. At this point the odds were very much on a draw. The crowd remained subdued. Lewis hovered inside the door of the bar, out of the sunlight, wearing a white shirt inscribed: "Lewis - best wishes, Anil Kumble." Many members were in shorts, toasting the hottest day of the year. At lunch I had seen a neatly dressed man arrive on a bicycle, wearing cycle clips and cuff links - metal at both sets of extremities.

At 213 for 5 Smith threw the ball to Darren Maddy, whose exuberant fielding had done much to lift his team's spirits in the field. Once - to save a run - he tore after a straight drive, and in one movement slid, stopped the ball, and hurled it back with a force that threw him flat on his back. But Maddy as a bowler, at such a critical juncture? This was a real gamble. He had taken only 20 first-class wickets in his whole career. Immediately, vindicating the ploy, he moved one enough to have Bowler lbw for 48, and for good measure bowled Parsons off his pads. It was 220 for 7, with just 48 overs left for play.

As the amount of playing time drained away, it seemed to be one of those occasions when wickets fell just too late for optimism. "It's going to be a thrash," said one member to another. Smith made yet another inspired change by bringing DeFreitas back to take Blackwell's wicket, but both DeFreitas and Ormond started to bowl wide of the wicket to the tail-enders. "They should stop bowling at first slip," muttered another spectator. In the end it was Kumble who finished things off with two lbw decisions. Somerset were out for 246, leaving Leicestershire 122 to win off 36 overs.

While Leicestershire were striving to get Somerset out, the assumption was that "the thrash" - as the member put it - would be something of a formality. As soon as Leicestershire started their innings, this had to be reconsidered, because 122 was a total big enough to permit a slip-up, and the scoring rate of 3.4 an over, though relatively modest, was well above the 2.5 an over sustained by both sides throughout the match. The target was put into perspective when Stevens again fell lbw to Rose, and Ward soon followed in the same way. Leicestershire were 8 for 2 after three overs.

" 'Ere we go again," said someone in the refreshment room. "We shall lose now," said one of the room's permanent residents to no-one in particular. "Thank you, Frank," said someone else, with great politeness.

Maddy had been out of runs so far in the season, but he began playing very positively. Smith joined him, in equally pugnacious mood. Now the game would be won or lost. Maddy sent two cover drives to the boundary, and Smith took another four to square leg. It was vivid, exciting cricket, and the crowd was uproariously appreciative of every run.

Two middle-aged ladies behind me, brought to the match by their husbands, missed all this. "Do they just have them in white?" one said. "Or in colours?" "No, in colours. They're such lovely doilies. On the corner of Brandon Street." Smith hooked Grove for four to make it 41 for 2 after 12 overs, and then Maddy drove straight for another boundary. "She asked me to ring and get her one," said the first lady. "I'd feel I was intruding, wouldn't you?"

Maddy snicked a four through the slips, and Smith drove two short deliveries from Blackwell through the covers for four. The Somerset fielders were still shouting to encourage each other. "They're not half-way yet," was a common cry. Then Maddy was bowled by Pierson for 39, to make the score 71 for 3. Surely Leicestershire could not lose it now? Habib settled in quickly, but departed lbw to Parsons. 94 for 4.

If doubts remained, they were soon settled by Dakin, coming in at fourth wicket down. For a couple of overs Smith had him 'scampering' quick singles. His 16-stone frame rebelled at this, and he wasted no time in striking the boundaries needed for a Leicestershire win. Each of his fine shots was greeted with relief and jubilation by members in the pavilion area, as the much-needed first win of the season was chalked up. This time, as he strode off to the pavilion between cheering ranks of spectators, Dakin's face broke into an enormous grin.

The match had been full of good things, with outstanding centuries from Habib and Trescothick, and excellent five-wicket spells from Rose, Grove and Kumble. But to my mind it belonged to John Dakin - a name that many cricket lovers may not know at all. Dakin had bowled well in the first innings, taking a couple of wickets, scored a magnificent century, and come in at the kill to finish off the match. He was popular with spectators, always referred to as 'John'. ("Hold on, John." "Well done, big John.") During the lunch interval of the third day he had been awarded his cap, after seven years with the county. I very much hoped that this time Leicestershire would not drop him, if and when Wells and Lewis returned to the team after injury.

Somerset first innings

ME Trescothick	c Maddy	b Kumble	105	**Bowling**	**O**	**M**	**R**	**W**
*J Cox	c Burns	b DeFreitas	8	Ormond	25	4	79	3
PCL Holloway	lbw	b Dakin	17	DeFreitas	24.5	10	49	3
PD Bowler	lbw	b Ormond	8	Kumble	26	9	62	2
M Burns	c Burns	b Ormond	4	Dakin	22	6	44	2
+RJ Turner		b Ormond	0	Crowe	4	0	19	0
KA Parsons	c Burns	b Dakin	20					
GD Rose	c Stevens	b DeFreitas	1					
ID Blackwell	c Burns	b Kumble	58					
ARK Pierson	c Burns	b DeFreitas	16					
JO Grove	not out		8					
Extras			17					
Total	All Out		**262**					

Leicestershire first innings

				Bowling	O	M	R	W
DI Stevens	lbw	b Rose	13	Bowling	O	M	R	W
DL Maddy		b Grove	5	Rose	34	11	74	5
TR Ward	lbw	b Rose	2	Grove	30.5	7	90	5
*BF Smith	c Parsons	b Rose	3	Parsons	12	3	41	0
A Habib	not out		172	Trescothick	8	0	50	0
JM Dakin	c Cox	b Grove	135	Blackwell	29	9	78	0
+ND Burns	c Turner	b Grove	6	Pierson	26	8	40	0
PAJ DeFreitas	c Burns	b Grove	0					
A Kumble	c Turner	b Rose	4					
CD Crowe	c Turner	b Rose	9					
J Ormond	lbw	b Grove	8					
Extras			30					
Total	All Out		387					

Somerset second innings

				Bowling	O	M	R	W
*J Cox	c Burns	b Kumble	24	Bowling	O	M	R	W
ME Trescothick	c Maddy	b Kumble	43	Ormond	21	4	58	0
PCL Holloway	c Burns	b DeFreitas	27	DeFreitas	27	11	48	3
PD Bowler	lbw	b Maddy	48	Kumble	38.2	12	61	5
M Burns		b DeFreitas	6	Crowe	5	1	12	0
+RJ Turner	lbw	b Kumble	15	Dakin	18	7	27	0
KA Parsons		b Maddy	25	Maddy	4	2	10	2
GD Rose	lbw	b Kumble	2					
ID Blackwell	c Burns	b DeFreitas	19					
ARK Pierson	not out		1					
JO Grove	lbw	b Kumble	0					
Extras			36					
Total	All Out		246					

Leicestershire second innings

				Bowling	O	M	R	W
DI Stevens	lbw	b Rose	3	Bowling	O	M	R	W
DL Maddy		b Pierson	39	Rose	9	1	28	2
TR Ward	lbw	b Rose	0	Grove	7	0	26	0
*BF Smith	not out		45	Blackwell	2	0	15	0
A Habib	lbw	b Parsons	9	Pierson	6	0	18	1
JM Dakin	not out		19	Parsons	5.5	0	28	1
Extras			9					
Total	4 wickets		124					

Leicestershire won by 6 wickets. Points: Leicestershire 19, Somerset 4

Aftab Habib leaving the field after his innings of 173 not out versus Somerset.
(Photo: Sylvia Michael)

The entrance to Grace Road (Photo: David Spiller)

4. Leicestershire versus Hampshire
Grace Road, 17 to 20 May

This was a depressing match, characterised by cold, poor weather, interruptions, and slow scoring. The plain facts of the game are easily told. In their first innings, Hampshire scored 229 and Leicestershire 289. In their second innings Hampshire reached 123 for 8 wickets before proceedings were mercifully brought to a close. The rates of scoring in these three innings were, respectively: 2.4 runs per over, 2.2, and 2.1.

The weather was atrocious throughout, with dark clouds scudding overhead, periodically interrupting play with drizzle or downpours or bad light. The players had no chance to settle. Not surprisingly the crowds were tiny; among the die-hards, overcoats and sweaters were out in force.

In the conditions, it was hard for the players to create memorable moments. Much of the press interest had been concentrated on the appearance of Australian Test spinner Shane Warne for Hampshire. He managed to score his first runs of the season (in five innings), greeted with ironic applause from his team-mates in the pavilion. More to the point, he took his first five-wicket haul of the season, bowling more than 40 overs for his team. It was fascinating to compare Warne's style with that of Kumble, the world's other outstanding leg-spin bowler. Warne's approach to the wicket has none of the taut, electric bustle of his rival. He stands menacingly still a few paces from the wicket, tossing the ball up, before executing a puddeny amble up to the crease and an undistinguished over-arm movement - but this is buttressed by the reputation of an assassin. Like Kumble, he keeps the batsmen guessing all the time. Habib - when well set - was lured out of his crease by the tantalising length, and very well stumped by Aymes. "Well done", said Warne, music to any wicket-keeper's ears. DeFreitas was completely undone by a fast, low ball which hit the stumps long before his bat descended to try and stop it. Sadly, Kumble was caught at the wicket off Mascarenhas before Warne had a chance to get after him.

In the circumstances, just as interesting as the play was seeing Warne in the restaurant area with the other Hampshire players, waiting for lunch, half-watching the England versus Zimbabwe Test match on a television set, making calls on a mobile phone, bonding with his team-mates, and dealing patiently with elderly autograph vultures - who almost make a business out of the monikers of the famous.

37

The Leicestershire innings was held together by Habib and Burns, scoring 66 and 69 respectively. Habib's long innings was all the more meritorious for being scored over eight separate passages of weather-disrupted play - no way for any batsman to build an innings. Burns was making his first real contribution for Leicestershire with the bat. Understandably, after three years out of the first-class game, he had looked quite rusty in the first few matches. There had been some rumblings among spectators, always cautious about newcomers. (" 'E's no swop for Nixon, is 'e"?) Burns was still having some trouble keeping to Kumble, whom he let through for four byes twice in this match, but some class strokes in this innings showed why he had a first-class average of 30, with four centuries to his credit.

Leicestershire pride themselves on producing good cricket pitches, but this season's crop was causing concern. Habib, fielding in the outfield during Hampshire's first innings, made his views felt to the groundsman, who was in the public seating near the scoreboard.

"It's slower than last week's," he called out. "I can't do any more to 'em". "I reckon the whole thing should be ripped up and start again."

The groundsman muttered unhappily to his side kick about this exchange, but I felt that DeFreitas would have had even less temperate views on the pitch. At three o'clock on that first day DeFreitas had tried a bouncer - the first of the season that I could recall on the Grace Road pitches. The batsman scornfully watched it go past.

At the close of play one image summed up the match. The groundsman's tractor drove onto the pitch with headlights blazing in the gloom.

It was all too clear throughout the last day that the match had died, and the crowd was tiny. All the same, those who did turn up followed play religiously. There is a spot in the bar where you can comfortably watch the game and the Test match on television. I did this as Graeme Hick reached a century against his old country, but my only companion was a small boy. The crowd's allegiance was local.

Just before tea there was just a moment when a Leicestershire victory seemed conceivable. Hampshire's fourth wicket fell at 67, and a couple of quick wickets then might have led to another last-hour thrash for victory by the home team. I was in the refreshment room at the time, but few of the residents paid any attention: some were asleep, others reading newspapers, and a small group was deep in discussion about some non-cricketing matter. The moment passed, and Hampshire easily held out for the draw. Two more hours of play would probably have meant a Leicestershire victory, but time lost to the weather ruined the match. The only consolation for Leicestershire was that most other county matches had been similarly affected. Despite winning just one match, they found themselves second in the Championship table. This said a good deal about the lottery of cricket and the weather.

Hampshire first innings

				Bowling	O	M	R	W
JS Laney		b DeFreitas	8	Bowling	O	M	R	W
DA Kenway	c Maddy	b Kumble	30	DeFreitas	20.3	6	36	3
WS Kendall	lbw	b DeFreitas	4	Dakin	18.4	4	49	1
*RA Smith	c Burns	b Boswell	26	Wells	11.3	3	30	1
GW White	lbw	b Kumble	0	Kumble	27	4	53	2
+AN Aymes	not out		74	Boswell	12	3	40	1
AD Mascarenhas	c Burns	b DeFreitas	8	Maddy	6	1	12	2
SK Warne		b Maddy	16					
SD Udal	c Burns	b Maddy	7					
SJ Renshaw	c Maddy	b Wells	26					
PJ Hartley	c Stevens	b Dakin	7					
Extras			23					
Total	All Out		**229**					

Leicestershire first innings

				Bowling	O	M	R	W
DL Maddy	lbw	b Hartley	22	Bowling	O	M	R	W
DI Stevens	lbw	b Warne	19	Hartley	29	5	70	2
TR Ward	st Aymes	b Warne	1	Renshaw	23	7	47	1
BF Smith	lbw	b Mascarenhas	32	Warne	43	13	86	5
A Habib	st Aymes	b Warne	66	Mascarenhas	19	4	33	2
*VJ Wells	c Aymes	b Hartley	2	Udal	15	5	35	0
JM Dakin	lbw	b Warne	36					
+ND Burns	not out		67					
PAJ DeFreitas		b Warne	0					
A Kumble	c Aymes	b Mascarenhas	2					
SAJ Boswell	c Aymes	b Renshaw	14					
Extras			28					
Total	All Out		**289**					

Hampshire second innings

				Bowling	O	M	R	W
JS Laney	c Ward	b Boswell	14	Bowling	O	M	R	W
DA Kenway		b DeFreitas	5	DeFreitas	21	7	41	4
WS Kendall	c Burns	b Kumble	8	Boswell	7	2	23	1
*RA Smith	c Ward	b Kumble	31	Dakin	3	1	8	0
GW White	lbw	b Wells	6	Kumble	22	7	27	2
+AN Aymes		b DeFreitas	13	Wells	5	2	8	1
AD Mascarenhas	c Wells	b DeFreitas	10	Maddy	2	1	2	0
SK Warne	not out		11					
SD Udal	c Dakin	b DeFreitas	1					
SJ Renshaw	not out		2					
Extras			22					
Total	8 wickets		**123**					

Match drawn. Points: Leicestershire 9, Hampshire 8

Grace Road: The pavilion and members' area seen from the Bennett end
(Photo: Neville Chadwick Photography)

Grace Road from the pavilion - with rain again. (Photo: Sylvia Michael)

5. Durham versus Leicestershire
Chester-le-Street, 24 to 27 May

Durham are the only new entrants to the County Championship in recent memory and, travelling north on the first morning of their match with Leicestershire, I was expecting to find some departures from tradition. The county ground is not in Durham itself (the only one not in a major city), but in the small town of Chester-le-Street (pronounced locally as "Chest-lee-street") - a 20-minute bus ride away, followed by a 15-minute walk. This is a facility marketed at motorists.

One eye-opener is the size of the ground. The club has aspirations. A truly enormous pitch lies at the centre of a great bowl of low seating, above and beyond which can be seen the Northumberland countryside, with houses on hilltops, Lumley castle, and the spire of Chester-le-Street church. Along one side of the pitch stands a very large pavilion and seating area for members, and a range of hospitality boxes. The small stands and other facilities for casual visitors are spick and span, though the area behind the scoreboard looks unfinished, housing an abandoned Kenco coffee stall and other stuff on wheels - like a dump for disbanded floats at a carnival.

Daily entrance to the ground is a mere £5, much lower than the £8-£10 charged at other grounds I had visited - and in contrast to the Durham membership fee, which is the most expensive of all the counties.

I had just come from the centre of Durham, a place where the large and very visible student population makes it unusual to see anyone over the age of 25 on the streets. Odd, then, to find that the cricket ground was populated almost exclusively by the old and retired. It was as if the two age groups had been forcibly segregated by some higher authority, while anyone aged between 25 and 60 had been sent off to work in farms, offices and factories, only to be glimpsed at weekends.

I had missed the pre-lunch session. Leicestershire, having won the toss and batted, were already 91 for 4. Only Darren Maddy had prospered and, after reaching 50 in the over after lunch with a straight boundary, he was comprehensively bowled by Melvyn Betts. Compared to Grace Road's flat track, the Chester-le-Street pitch looked very different. Ten minutes after I arrived, Durham's John Wood nearly decapitated Dakin with a bouncer. Bouncers! I had almost forgotten they existed. Recent press coverage had speculated about low totals on Durham's pitches, and the crowd were clearly expecting more of the same. "If you can get 200 on the board, you stand a chance," said someone.

Leicestershire were a long way from that happy position. Apart from bounce, the pitch encouraged each-way movement, and many shots flew off the edge of the bat in directions unintended. The Durham side is noted for its seam bowling. Though two of their biggest wicket takers, Simon Brown and Neil Killeen, were missing, they offered resources enough in Wood, Betts, and Steve Harmison, plus a young player in his first season - Ian Hunter.

Harmison had been in the England 13 for the first Test against Zimbabwe two weeks earlier, and rumours that he was 'seriously fast' had sparked a lot of interest. He was quick all right. This latest English hope was 21-years-old, and six feet four inches tall; and as was now apparent, had a very solid 14-stone frame. He came in off a shortish, relaxed run, but the ball reached the batsman at quite a lick, often rising outside the off stump. In a sense this constituted a weakness, as many of Harmison's thunderballs could be left alone. It was when the batsman made to play them that their problems occurred. The next wicket fell when Wells hooked at a short delivery, skied the ball, and was very well caught by Betts, running in from mid-wicket and diving full length almost onto the strip. Leicestershire were 128 for 6.

In their awkward position Leicestershire's scoring rate was understandably slow, as Dakin and Chris Lewis set about rebuilding. Nick Speak, the Durham captain, rotated his hand of seam bowlers. Lewis was quiescent, and Dakin scored in twos and threes rather than his usual currency of boundaries. The massive playing area at Durham meant that shots which would normally have made the ropes were often pulled up by fielders. With all the boundaries equidistant, I found that I longed for a short one, to give the game added interest.

A spectator echoed another thought when he lamented "Our bowling is much of a muchness"; Durham have good seamers of the fast-medium kind, Harmison excepted, but lack variety. When Speak turned to his fifth bowler, Collingwood, he too turned out to be a seamer. And then, to a flurry of excitement in the stands, Speak called into action Durham's overseas player, Simon Katich. And Katich was a spinner. The reaction suggested that something unusual was running in to bowl - a rhinoceros, say, or a rare species of warthog. I looked him up in the *Playfair Cricket Annual*. He had a career wicket-bag of three, at an average of 81 each. Nevertheless he bowled a couple of keenly watched maiden overs before, in his third, Lewis heaved at him and was bowled - by Katich's Chinaman, according to press reports the next day. Astonishment all round. "Well, well, well," said my neighbour. "Secret weapon."

Soon after this Burns went too, and at tea Leicestershire were in deep grief at 167 for 8. During the interval I asked a spectator what was considered a good score on Durham's pitches. He thought that 200 would be satisfactory for the Leicestershire team, but that if Durham got them out for 180 the home team would have done well. Thus finely are matters judged in these parts. I asked him if Durham had ever had a spinner before Katich.

"Spinner?" he said, screwing up his features and searching his memory, as if for some long-extinct organism, dimly remembered from childhood. "I think there is one in the second team."

The Durham spectators were obviously expecting to watch their team bat that evening, but after tea Dakin and DeFreitas began building a stand. For his captain, DeFreitas must be a nightmare to place in a batting order. Here he was coming in at number 10 - his rightful place, if recent scores were taken into account - and immediately batting with a calm certainty warranting a much higher position.

Dakin, for the third match in succession, was building an innings - something he had often been accused of failing to do. What impressed in this match was the quality of his behind-the-wicket strokes. In his big century against Somerset almost every intentional run had been scored from drives in front of the wicket. Now, when he swept very fine for four immediately after tea, it was his first run behind the wicket that I could recall. But not the last. He followed it with a late cut for a single, a square drive for two, and a fierce cut for four. When he reached his half-century off 133 balls, it included only two boundaries, a sure sign of circumspection from a man who normally dealt in fours and sixes.

His 50 was generously applauded by Durham spectators, despite obstructing their aspirations. They were the quietest crowd encountered so far, fair and knowledgeable. But bad fielding particularly bothered them. One or two misfields brought the biggest crowd reaction of the day. And as for overthrows! There was only one, but it drew from members in the pavilion a deep, Greek-chorus of a groan, as if from men broken by some utterly tragic piece of news.

Tea had been taken at 167 for 8 and, given the interval prognostication of "a good score" on this pitch, the evening passage of play assumed peculiar significance. Dakin and DeFreitas pushed on with great difficulty. At 189 DeFreitas was dropped off a high, hard chance to the gulley. Dakin was hit painfully on the body by Hunter then, shaping to hook Harmison and misjudging his pace, played a strange kind of forward defensive shot chest high. Another elegant leg glance and a fierce cut both went for four, reinforcing his behind-the-wicket ability. I was astonished that I had only now noticed Dakin's habit, when batting, of shooting his left arm skywards, like a member of the Third Reich enacting a *"Heil Hitler"*.

DeFreitas was also picking up ones and twos, and a single from him sent Leicestershire's total to 250, off 98 overs, and the partnership to 83. Only now did Durham, for the first time in the innings, post a forward short leg. Frustration swelled off the pitch, among a crowd apparently resigned to their team surrendering the initiative.

"It's just deplorable." "They're not making it happen." "At 97 for 5 we were hopefully goin' to wrap it up." "We do make it hard for ourselves, don't we."

Just as he was pushing for his century Dakin lost the strike, and spent several overs without facing. When he did get back he immediately played on to Wood, out for 89. A trade-mark of his is the slow, feet-dragging return to the pavilion after getting out, and he looked especially sad here following such an anti-climactic dismissal. Durham's crowd gave generous applause, but the Leicestershire players out-did them. There are few supporters for away teams in cricket, and the players take over the role. As the crowd's clapping died away, applause from the Leicestershire players swelled raucously, accompanying Dakin into the pavilion.

Leicestershire ended the day on 256, with their last wicket pair together - DeFreitas on 31, and Carl Crowe on 3. If the tea-time information had been correct, this was already a good score.

Second day

Next morning, the Leicestershire innings was not expected to last long. Carl Crowe had played a handful of first class innings, with a top score of 44 not out, and was likely to hold an end up rather than play strokes. But Leicestershire are good at last wicket partnerships. They bat through the order, and delight in those aggravating, impermanent stands which wind up the opposition and raise their own morale. DeFreitas was playing like the first-rate county batsman he was once thought to be. He brought up his own 50 with a very fine cover drive, and went on to pull, cut and drive the opposition into deep depression. At one point Durham had five fielders on the boundary to him. At long last, after an hour-and-a-half's play, Harmison trapped Crowe lbw bang in front of the stumps, to a relieved roar from most of the Durham team. Crowe was so palpably out that a spectator observed "That was a waste of cheer". Leicestershire were all out for 336, and had - to the disbelief of people in the crowd - doubled their score for the last two wickets. DeFreitas remained unbeaten on 81.

Durham spectators, though highly supportive of their team, were also going through a crisis of confidence. Back when the score was 230, someone had wailed "We can't get 230 runs - we haven't the batsmen". As they waited for the Durham openers to appear, their concern erupted into a clamour of apprehension.

"Suddenly the pitch'll be extremely dangerous." "We've only got one batsman in form."

Some very dark clouds were looming over the pavilion, and someone else, anticipating rain, said lugubriously: "At least we won't lose".

In fact Durham's openers, Jonathan Lewis and James Daley, proceeded untroubled to the interval. When Lewis sent a fierce square cut for four, relief burst out in the loudest applause of the match. At lunch they were 30 for no wicket.

"Best opening stand of the year." "Sshhhh!."

Durham's geography seems to lend itself to remarkable transformations in the weather. At lunch the clouds were dark, but high in the sky. I came out of the cafe twenty minutes later to find that a kind of sea fret had descended upon the ground, bringing a scene of utter bleakness, the wicket covered by all the paraphernalia of wet conditions, the surrounding stands deserted, and spectators dispersed like a conjuror's rabbits. There was clearly no prospect of play for some time.

On a nice day, the Durham ground has an airy, open feel, but it lacks cover. There is one rather posh cafe, but the only other place to get out of the rain is the back of the pavilion area, and it was here that rows of weather-hardened spectators stood in the wind, up against the concrete and red-brick walls, as if waiting to be shot. Durham do not offer a museum for spectators to wander round in wet weather. A few people stayed in their seats, covering themselves with very large umbrellas, but most just 'disappeared'.

Two hours passed before there was movement in this scene of desolation, and then the old rituals of reviving a cricket match began again. The rain stopped, and a watery sun peered through. A remote cheer came from the pavilion as a row of ground staff began pulling at the first cover. The familiar equipment of tractors and rollers appeared, three linked sets of covers were towed away like barges on a canal, and the green carpets rolled up. Life returned to the stands, as if after hibernation: figures emerged, stretching, from umbrellas, the cafe emptied, and people drifted in from cars parked on the perimeters. Finally at 3.40pm, with sun beating down, came a rare announcement. "Play will resume at 4.20pm."

"They *must* have their tea," said a man through gritted teeth - and not without cause. Tea was clearly the reason the players were not out at 4pm - after a two-hour rest sufficient to consume buckets of tea, and a four-course meal as well.

To his credit, DeFreitas was down on the edge of the pitch at four o'clock, as if warming up for a first bowl. Perhaps this was a case of virtue rewarded for, coming in from the opposite end to his pre-lunch spell, he soon bowled Lewis with a ball which came back and kept low, then had Daley well caught by Maddy low at cover. The certainty of Durham's opening stand had dissipated, and DeFreitas claimed Collingwood's wicket too with a length ball that moved away from him. Durham were 52 for 3.

'Daffy's' commitment to his new county (or rather, his former county) was impressive. At 34 years old he was a candidate for the 'old lags' category, but had bowled with great skill and enthusiasm throughout the early season, taken a lot of wickets, and was already the only Leicestershire quick bowler to have stayed fit. Today he had taken his score to more than 80, bowled 13 overs, and taken three wickets. Even the Durham supporters gave him a round of applause as he trudged down to long leg, though one of them, watching his twisting and gyrating exercises between overs called out "Twist it a bit more".

Leicestershire had a bowling problem. Their speed-man, Ormond, was still out with injury, and Kumble had been unexpectedly whisked away by India for the Asia Cup. Lewis was carrying an injury, bowling from a shortened run-up. It was still enough to knock down the stumps of Speak, playing rather indeterminately forward. Lewis was immediately taken off, as if his captain had promised him a rest in return for a wicket. But Leicestershire is a team, and the players cover for one another. There were spells from Dakin, Wells and Maddy, and 10 minutes before the close Wells put on the young spinner, Carl Crowe. In his first over Crowe bowled Nick Peng, an even younger player who had caused much excitement with his recent 98 against Surrey. Peng was the eighth player to be bowled, out of 14 dismissals so far in the match.

Crowe should perhaps have been tried earlier in the innings, and did not want to miss his chance now. At the end of the penultimate over DeFreitas advanced from long leg pulling off his sweater, calling "Can I have the last one?", but Crowe strode in very purposefully, looking straight ahead, and got there first. At the close, Durham were in trouble at 82 for 5, though Katich had played well for 28 not out. Going into the pavilion the Leicestershire players - again both performers and supporters - formed an avenue and cheered DeFreitas off, after his brilliant day.

That evening I tried to get reports of other county matches on Radio 5live. There was a 5-second headline comment on just one of them, preceded by a report lasting several minutes (including an interview) on the condition of footballer Andy Cole's toe. Small wonder that football increasingly pushes cricket onto the margins of sporting news. To argue that the media only gives the public what it wants would be naive, because the media heavily influences what the public wants

Third day

The third day of the match began under an overcast sky, echoing an atrocious forecast for the country as a whole. "I think we'll get a couple of showers," observed a spectator with extreme optimism.

The Leicestershire players were in high spirits in the field, with Maddy playfully trying to scale the heights of John Dakin; but Durham, teetering on the brink of 82 for 5, took the early honours. On the face of it the batsmen were an ill-matched pair: Simon Katich was, according to a spectator, "the only Durham batsman in form", while Ian Hunter had been promoted from number 10 on the scoresheet to act as night watchman. DeFreitas had an early indication that this was not to be his day when he sauntered to the ball at long leg, allowing the batsmen to run three. Katich hit DeFreitas himself for three through the covers, then Hunter took three off the front foot through mid-wicket, and another three straight. The number of 'threes' in the match - and presumably every match here - was a comment on the extraordinary size of the playing area; retrieving a hit from the outfield was the equivalent of a country walk.

Liberated from the flat Grace Road pitches, the Leicestershire bowlers were all rediscovering the art of the bouncer, like children with new toys. From one of these, Hunter executed a thrilling hook shot. Now the crowd really sat up and took notice. Hunter, in his first season, was an unknown. Had Durham discovered an all-rounder?

Nevertheless, Katich was the main hope. The Ladbroke's bookmakers stall on the ground had quoted 11/4 odds on Katich for the top Durham innings, well ahead of Speak and Lewis at 9/2 and Hunter at 50/1. They obviously knew a thing or two. Katich already had the top score, and was not to relinquish that position. He had a first class average well over 50, yet was nowhere near the Australian Test team. Something you noticed about him, as with nearly all Australian batsmen, is the way his electric running turned singles into twos, and twos into threes - and you also wondered why all English batsmen cannot emulate this.

Leicestershire posted three slips *and* a third man to the faster bowlers (a sensible but rarely seen combination), and the Durham pair scored quickly. Katich had all the strokes, and in quick order displayed a cover drive, cut, leg glance and pull - all for boundaries. When he reached his 50, off 126 balls, the helmet came off to reveal newly dyed flaxen hair.

Hunter's innings was sublime and ridiculous. He tried frequent, extravagant drives outside the off stump without connecting, and between times played some strokes worthy of the best. A front foot cover drive off Wells brought cries of appreciation from the dour Durham crowd, and was followed by an even better stroke to the same area, timed so the ball raced to the distant boundary. Nearing 50, he was fortunate to have Katich as his partner, as a straight drive resulted in an all-run four and his debut half century. The crowd erupted as if greeting the second coming.

Katich pulled Dakin violently for four to bring up the 100 partnership. Durham were 182 for 5. Though Wells is good at pressuring batsmen through fielding adjustments, his bowling changes can be unimaginative, almost running through the cast list in order of seniority. Despite taking a wicket the previous evening, Crowe only appeared at 12.45pm, when Durham were already 190 for 5.

At ten past one the 200 came up, off 73 overs, with Katich on 89 and Hunter on 54. Heavy, black clouds signified all too clearly that the 'sea fret' was again about to interrupt play, and it became a matter of whether Katich could reach his century first. Spectators were watching the umpires like hawks, and at the first sign of a light meter came the cry: "Come on, put that away. You'll get your wages anyway."

It was a close-run thing. Katich went down the pitch to strike DeFreitas straight for four, bring up his 100 (201 balls, 11 fours), and the partnership to 140. Almost immediately the players turned towards the pavilion. The covers went on, and the rain descended, reprising the mournful scene of the previous day. This time there was to be no late-afternoon reprieve. The departure of the ice-cream van, around 2.30pm, signified the end of play for the day.

Fourth day

On the last day, which was truncated and meaningless, Durham reached 302 for 8 wickets, with Katich unbeaten on 137. Their late declaration deprived Leicestershire of the chance of pursuing an extra bonus point.

All the same - since play had been abandoned everywhere else as well - the points accrued were enough to lift Leicestershire to a surprising top-of-the-table position, albeit from more games than other teams. The table was fairly meaningless at this stage of the season, because so few games had finished, and the paltry totals registered had been scraped together from bonus points. I had seen all five Leicestershire matches, three of them irretrievably ruined by the weather. If one could imagine three out of five professional football matches being abandoned at half-time (or more to the point, abandoned after keeping spectators waiting for two hours), and the effect that this would have on football attendance figures, the patience of cricket followers can be seen in perspective.

The match had been dominated by Dakin and DeFreitas for Leicestershire, and Katich and Hunter for Durham, a combination which suggested which kinds of players were needed for teams to be successful in a County Championship season. Current, top-of-the-bill performers need not apply, because they are likely to be whisked away to Test duty for England (playing seven Test matches in the Summer of 2000) or, in the case of overseas players, to play for their countries in international events like the Asia Cup. What counties need are players just over the top of the international hill (but not far down the slope on the other side), others not

49

quite good enough for regular Test duty, and others good enough but also young enough to be starting up the hill - or (like John Dakin) good county players who have rediscovered themselves, but not been discovered by anyone else.

Leicestershire first innings

DI Stevens	c Collingwood	b Betts	10
DL Maddy		b Betts	50
TR Ward		b Harmison	0
BF Smith	c Collingwood	b Wood	14
A Habib	lbw	b Wood	11
*VJ Wells	c Betts	b Harmison	17
JM Dakin		b Wood	89
CC Lewis		b Katich	9
+ND Burns	lbw	b Betts	1
PAJ DeFreitas	not out		81
CD Crowe	lbw	b Harmison	21
Extras			33
Total	All Out		**336**

Bowling	O	M	R	W
Harmison	30.3	9	61	3
Betts	33	4	73	3
Hunter	22	4	66	0
Wood	30	2	89	3
Collingwood	4	0	7	0
Katich	10	1	25	1

Durham first innings

JJB Lewis		b DeFreitas	25
JA Daley	c Maddy	b DeFreitas	16
SM Katich	not out		137
PD Collingwood		b DeFreitas	2
*NJ Speak		b Lewis	1
N Peng		b Crowe	4
ID Hunter	st Burns	b Crowe	63
+MP Speight	c Maddy	b Dakin	12
J Wood	lbw	b Crowe	26
MM Betts	not out		0
Extras			16
Total	8 wickets declared		**302**

Bowling	O	M	R	W
DeFreitas	38	9	99	3
Lewis	20	2	50	1
Dakin	20	4	55	1
Wells	12	2	42	0
Maddy	8	5	11	0
Crowe	19.2	8	33	3

Match Drawn. Points: Durham 10, Leicestershire 9

6. Yorkshire versus Leicestershire
Headingley, 31 May to 3 June

At Durham I had arrived at lunchtime and found Leicestershire 90 for 4, with Darren Maddy on 46. At Headingley I was only 40 minutes late at the ground, and found Leicestershire already 52 for no wicket, with Maddy again making the running, and well into his 30s.

Leicestershire had reorganised their batting order, with Ward opening alongside Maddy, and Stevens dropping to number six. Out of the side were Kumble, Dakin (injured) and Lewis - pulled out with 'a hip injury and back spasms' *(plus ca change)*; in were Sutcliffe, Osmond and Boswell.

Leicestershire's injury problems were as nothing against Yorkshire's. They had both Michael Vaughan and McGrath missing from their batting line-up, along with four noted quick bowlers: Darren Gough, on Test duty; Craig White, who had blacked out in the street that week; and Silverwood and Sidebottom, both injured. Not for nothing do people talk of a 'seamer factory' at Leeds. Yorkshire still managed to field Gavin Hamilton (he of the one Test appearance), two players spoken of as Test hopefuls, Paul Hutchison and Matthew Hoggard (Hoggard to become more than "a hopeful" before the end of the season), and a newcomer - 19-year old Chris Elstub. The absence of established players was a sore point with some spectators: "If we can't get bloody Test players ter cum dahn 'ere, go a'ead with youngsters."

Maddy was going like a train. I gathered that he had taken advantage of loose, leg-side bowling in the early overs. As I arrived he deflected a ball through the slips for four (something he is very good at), and in successive balls struck twos through the off-side. He brings to batting all the positive aspects of his fielding. Hoggard and Hamilton were bowling; Hoggard, coming in off a much shorter run than his team-mate, looked distinctly quicker and more threatening.

Maddy cut for four, bringing up his half century off a mere 57 balls. Ward looked much less settled and at 24 hung his bat outside off stump to Hamilton and was taken by Byas at slip. Ward's irritated gesture revealed how badly things had gone for him so far on his move to the Midlands. And Leicestershire were 84 for 1.

As the array of quicker bowlers on both sides attested, Headingley is noted as a seamer's wicket, but Yorkshire now brought on an off-spinner.

51

James Middlebrook, 23-years-old, had made his debut for the county in 1998 but not played at all in 1999. Maddy went down the wicket to strike him over the top; then he and Wells took four singles off the same over, taking Leicestershire to 100 for 1. "Nothing there at all," said a spectator. "Playin' 'im wi' ease, aren't they?"

Almost immediately Middlebrook turned one to have Maddy caught at slip by Byas, falling as he took it. This was so unexpected, and against the natural order of things, that for the time being it knocked the stuffing out of Leicestershire's innings. The scoring rate plummeted. Lunch was taken at 113 for 3 off 36 overs.

Here was my first opportunity to walk round the ground. Headingley is not everyone's favourite cricket venue but, on a pleasant, sunny day, with a substantial crowd in, it had a pleasing aspect. Nearly half the ground is set aside for members, and the other half crammed with the deep banks of seating necessary to accommodate Test match crowds. As with Chester-le-Street, there is nowhere to find cover, from sun or rain. English cricket grounds are capable of infinite variations, and the unusual feature here is a broad road running round most of the pitch perimeter. The only traffic on this Appian Way was a small trolley, absurdly clattered along the hard surface every day at lunch time by two girls on the catering staff, with much jangling of crockery.

During lunch spectators could buy second-hand books from a stall on the boundary. There was also a hot dog stall but, as at Old Trafford, there was nowhere I could find to buy a sandwich. Several hundred people in the non-members' seating and no sandwiches! I record this from a sense of disbelief.

The ground sprawls in surprising directions. At the back of the public seating a path runs alongside a row of dishevelled back gardens attached to red-brick houses - a strangely informal scene to find in a major stadium. At the end of the path is another pitch, surrounded by substantial stands: the Leeds Rugby League ground.

After lunch, I got my first sight of Paul Hutchison, coming in from the pavilion end. Though only 22-years- old, he had already taken 132 first class wickets at the very low cost of 22.1 runs each - an average which put him second (after Saqlain Mushtaq) in the list of all bowlers currently active in English county cricket. He is an unmistakable figure, tall, and very thin; with his fair, wavy hair and boyish enthusiasm, you could easily imagine Hutchison on the playing fields of some English public school. He also has one of the most instantly recognisable bowling actions: a high-stepping gait, left (delivery) arm held almost at right angles behind him, and an enormous leap at the crease. From where I sat he seemed to be leaning backwards on the run-in. He tended to skid the ball through, rarely gaining any bounce, and too many efforts went down the leg side, but there was aggression in abundance. It soon made Wells play on for 19.

Hamilton was on at the other end, bowling a lot of short-pitched stuff which Ben Smith hit several times for boundaries. Habib got going quickly, and the Leicestershire innings had regained much of its momentum when everything was turned upside down. As so often happens, it was a catch which made the difference. Darren Lehmann, Yorkshire's overseas player, was cannily stationed at short mid-wicket, and took a brilliant low effort off Habib to make Leicestershire 149 for 4. The innings never quite recovered from the loss of their best batsman. Stevens came in and, forcing the pace, was caught from a mis-hook, to give Elstub his first wicket in county cricket.

Middlebrook replaced Hutchison, and reinforced the good impression made earlier. He had taken over from Richard Stemp as the Yorkshire spinner, and I was reminded of a comment overheard in the Grace Road refreshment room. "I've seen Stemp bowl for Worcestershire, I've seen 'im bowl for Yorkshire, and now I've seen 'im bowl for Nottinghamshire - and I 'aven't seen 'im turn it yet." Middlebrook was turning it though. He had Smith dropped at slip before bowling him on the back foot. To show it was no fluke, he also got Burns to edge to slip, where Byas (to show *his* drop was no accident, let it go again). It made little difference because Hamilton, on for Elstub, knocked back Burns's stumps to a jubilant shout from the crowd. At 171 for 7, Leicestershire were falling apart.

DeFreitas came to the wicket, following his 80 at the tail-end of the innings at Chester-le-Street. Could he do it again? The first signs were encouraging, as he hooked a short ball from Middlebrook high to the square-leg boundary. At the other end Hoggard, thick-set and powerful, generated real pace from his shortish run-up, and had Sutcliffe lbw on the front foot. Then, against Ormond, he knocked two stumps out of the ground with a no-ball, to a gladiatorial roar from the pavilion - the sight of stumps flying inflaming the crowd.

Daffy played responsibly, starting off with ones and twos - always a good sign in his case. He seemed to be enjoying his batting. When in full flow, his range of strokes is as full as any class batsman. He deflected Hamilton for four to very fine leg, then sent him through the covers off the back foot. Ormond joined in with another fine deflection off Hutchison. There were groans from the crowd as the Leicestershire score mounted, and animal cries of pain from Blakey, the wicketkeeper, at a couple of near things. The weather echoed the change in play; Yorkshire's sunny day was ebbing away, and we were back to the cold, grey atmosphere which had become so familiar for the whole of May.

The 50 partnership was completed at 247, with DeFreitas on 45 and Ormond 15. DeFreitas again deflected a four to fine leg off Hamilton, who seemed to be a slow learner. Daffy's half century was scored off 79 balls. It took Middlebrook, returning, to break the partnership, by bowling Ormond on the forward stroke. Leicestershire 257 for 9.

It was not over yet. Boswell came in to join DeFreitas for the last wicket, and Daffy smashed Elstub to the mid-wicket boundary, then advanced yards down the pitch to the same bowler (considerably sharper than medium pace) to bang him through the covers. The batsmen momentarily fell asleep when Lehmann replaced Elstub - spinners from both ends at Headingley - and reawoke when Hamilton took the new ball. The first over with it went for 14. Hutchison put an end to the fun, bowling DeFreitas as he attempted the boundary which would have brought up Leicestershire's 300. The roar of exultation from the crowd revealed how much these partnerships for the last two wickets - comprising exactly 100 runs - had got on their nerves.

As I left the ground a man was saying to his uncomprehending, ankle-socked young daughter: "I'd say two sessions to Leicestershire and one to Yorkshire". His judgement summed it up neatly.

Second day

One look out of the window on the morning of the second day was enough to show that the wretched bad weather was back again. Amazingly, after much drizzle in the early part of the morning, play started only ten minutes late. The elements had taken their toll on gate receipts, and the big public seating areas were almost empty. I sat among a small knot of regulars, as Yorkshire as Yorkshire pudding. The man next to me, the outspoken type, was square in shape, with pugnacious set of jaw. He and his companions were outraged when one of the umpires gave Craven lbw to Ormond early in the play.

" 'Ow the 'ell could 'e give that?" "Look where 'is front foot is."

"They weren't givin' em yesterday." "A Yorkshire League umpire wouldn't 've given that."

The incident gave rise to a prolonged discussion of umpires and their failings. Someone reported on a snooker umpire who had been interviewed on television the previous evening. " 'E said "I've 'ad ter give it up. Ah can't see end of the table now"'.

A second shout rang out from the Leicestershire fielders, and the square man erupted in irritation. "Will you shut up shoutin'."

Fortunately this appeal was declined, pre-empting apoplexy among a whole row of spectators. It dawned on me that making an appeal against a Yorkshireman was improper, while upholding an appeal was a crime against humanity. Just as the mutterings were dying down a newcomer arrived in my row and revived them, by enquiring how Craven had been out.

"'E was lbw - *well*, umpire give 'im."

" 'E's a poor umpire," said the square man. "We've 'ad 'im abaht four times this season already."

Another violent appeal was turned down, this time by umpire Shepherd. The square man responded immediately.

"Now Shepherd - 'e's a good umpire. That idiot at square leg..."

Shortly afterwards, even the first umpire turned one down too.

"'E's bin watchin' Shepherd. 'E knows what ter do now."

In stark contrast to the previous day's play, Yorkshire were making very slow progress against the bowling of DeFreitas and Ormond. After an hour, they had 16 runs off 17 overs. This was too much for even the most phlegmatic of spectators - "There's nowt goin' on 'ere" - and they turned to their lunch boxes. The square man folded a chocolate wrapper over and over into a tiny rectangle. Leicestershire's Boswell came on to bowl, reviving ancient local loyalties. "A Yorkshire lad, ain't 'e?" "Aye."

Blakey was lbw playing no stroke, a factor which this time muted the protests, and the Australian Darren Lehmann came out, in the middle of a fine run of form. He immediately found runs where none had existed before, turning Wells comfortably to square leg for two, and taking two more through the covers. Another cover drive for four was followed by a lovely deflection wide of gully for three.

"My money's on 'im," said someone. "There's always summat 'appenin' when 'e's there."

But the group's reaction to this opinion was rather half-hearted. It was good that Lehmann was scoring runs for Yorkshire, of course; but against that, he was not a Yorkshireman.

The square man was cautious in his judgements about most things: "Ah've never bin very impressed by 'im," he said about DeFreitas.

During the course of the morning there was quite a list of people the square man had not been impressed by, including David Beckham, seen in an England football match on television the previous evening. Though he did not say so, I felt that he would not have been impressed by Jack Hobbs either, or by Don Bradman.

Unaware of doubts about his pedigree, Lehmann was playing a delightful, sunny innings - at odds with the dark clouds intensifying overhead. His angled deflections to third man were a special delight. Even Byas, who had been comatose all morning, woke up and hooked over square leg for his first four of the innings. At lunch, Yorkshire were 74 for 2, with Lehmann already on 32.

The after-lunch session, though short, was enough for Leicestershire to have one outrageous piece of luck. They were desperately short of bowling in this match, and their two strike bowlers had virtually been 'bowled out' in the morning session. Lehmann dominated utterly, and a century was his for the taking. When Ormond bowled again he tried to stop a Byas drive, and deflected the ball onto the stumps. Lehmann, backing up in pukka Australian fashion, was run out for 39.

The heavens wept at that. The players came off, and no further play took place for the rest of the day.

Third day

The third day dawned even more dull and overcast than the second, putting prospects of play in serious doubt. Spectators have a tricky decision to make on these occasions. Do they pay their £9, only to find play rained off after 10 minutes? If so, there is no prospect of a refund.

In the event, play in this match described a displeasingly symmetrical pattern: a full six hours on day one was followed by three hours on day two, one hour on day three, and no play at all on day four. The match was abandoned with Yorkshire on 107 for 4, in reply to Leicestershire's 296. A mere one and a half innings had been played, out of the necessary four.

Four of the six matches I had attended had now been rained off. Apart from ritual cursing at the English weather, the cricket spectator might also query the championship fixture list. Leicestershire had six matches by the end of May, and one fixture scheduled for June - when the weather (please God) was likely to improve. The sequence of fixtures also had a lopsided appearance, with Leicestershire playing two away, then two at home, then two more away. At Durham - the most northerly county, with arguably the worst weather prospects - supporters complained that their first three matches in May were at home. There is more sense in the football calendar, which in general alternates home and away matches throughout the season.

Leicestershire first innings

TR Ward	c Byas	b Hamilton	24	**Bowling**	**O**	**M**	**R**	**W**
DL Maddy	c Byas	b Middlebrook	63	Hoggard	21	6	55	1
*VJ Wells		b Hutchison	19	Hutchison	15.5	3	62	3
BF Smith	lbw	b Middlebrook	30	Hamilton	21	6	80	2
A Habib	c Lehmann	b Hutchison	6	Elstub	13	3	36	1
DI Stevens	c Craven	b Elstub	9	Middlebrook	22	9	39	3
IJ Sutcliffe	lbw	b Hoggard	14	Lehmann	9	2	15	0
+ND Burns		b Hamilton	6					
PAJ DeFreitas		b Hutchison	70					
J Ormond		b Middlebrook	20					
SAJ Boswell	not out		12					
Extras			23					
Total	All Out		**296**					

Yorkshire first innings

*D Byas	c Burns	b Boswell	44	**Bowling**	**O**	**M**	**R**	**W**
VJ Craven	lbw	b Ormond	1	Ormond	24	11	50	1
+RJ Blakey	lbw	b Wells	9	Boswell	9.4	3	18	1
DS Lehmann	run out		39	DeFreitas	23	6	40	0
MJ Wood	not out		17	Wells	6	1	25	1
GM Fellows	not out		19	Maddy	2	1	4	0
Extras			17					
Total	4 wickets		146					

Match drawn. Points: Yorkshire 7, Leicestershire 7

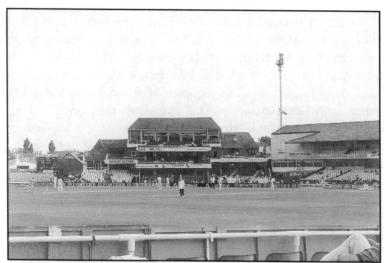

Headingley. A rugby league ground floodlight towers above the cricket.
(Photo: Peter David Lush)

Key equipment: Leicestershire's machine for clearing water
(Photo: Peter David Lush)

7. Leicestershire versus Derbyshire
Grace Road, 14 to 17 June

The first day of this match was rained off completely, emphasising Leicestershire's appalling luck with the weather this season. That said, the second and third days took place in the warmest weather of the year. It was sod's law that these were the only two days of Grace Road cricket that I missed during the summer. The Foxes made very good use of the fine weather. They won the toss and batted, reaching 310 all out - a total all the more impressive for being constructed from 57 for 4. Again Aftab Habib was the saviour, scoring 164 from 225 balls, with 21 fours and two sixes. He was supported by Sutcliffe and, once again, DeFreitas. On the third day the bowlers extracted full advantage from this platform. Ormond took six wickets as Derbyshire were bowled out for 133. They followed on and lost another five wickets in reaching 116 - still 61 runs behind.

This was the situation when I arrived early for the fourth and last sequence of play on another warm day. There was almost a holiday atmosphere for a session in which Leicestershire were expected to roll over the remnants of Derbyshire's batting order. The mower was out on a ground basking in sunshine, and several players lay prone on different parts of the grass surface, like bathers scattered on a beach. Entrance was free. I waved my membership card at the frail, grey-haired bouncer who guarded the members' area, but he was slumped over a newspaper.

"'E's too busy," called a second bouncer, walking past. "There's no charge today, so 'e's just 'aving a rest."

The 'bouncers' employed at the ground, distinguishable by their white coats, are well into retirement. In physical terms they might struggle to eject a well-built 10-year-old. Even more advanced in years is the old chap who guards the players' quarters from a stool just inside the door, his very antiquity a barrier to misbehaviour.

The advanced state of the match had not prevented a decent crowd from turning out to sit in the sunshine. Rows of deck chairs were in place. A number of women were elegantly dressed in summer outfits - not always matched by their companions, for whom shorts were by far the most popular option. Cheerleader Lewis was in a yellow batik shirt festooned with guitars and pineapples.

One of the wickets to have fallen the previous evening was the night watchman, so Derbyshire still had two batsmen to walk out at 11am: Titchard and Cassar. After the clatter of wickets on the previous day, all the talk among members was of a very short session this morning ("a formality," said one), but this was not quite how things turned out. True, the bails were disturbed four times in the first half hour, but by return throws on each occasion. The batsmen played confidently against Ormond and Kumble. Titchard struck a straight four, and Cassar turned Ormond very fine to the long leg boundary. Derbyshire were one short of their 150 when an Ormond bouncer surprised Titchard and ballooned into the air; Kumble, running in from gully, dived forward to take it just off the turf.

But the floodgates did not open at the fall of Titchard's wicket. Wicketkeeper Krikken came in to replace him and played soundly. Cassar's method against Kumble was to stand with bat raised and allow anything off the wicket to hit his pads - so much so that Lewis's voice was heard: "Hit the wicket. Mek 'im play."

Out of the blue, Cassar hit Kumble for six over long on, an indignity to which the Indian leg-spinner was definitely not accustomed. Further boundaries followed off both Lewis and Kumble. With Derbyshire on 187 for 6, I had a first, faint apprehension that they might after all save the match. Other Leicester members looked concerned. The wife of one said to another woman: "Thought we'd be done by now, didn't you?", not quite with a sigh, but as though there were lawns to be cut and shopping to be done.

I was standing by the pavilion, and noted the useful role played by another white-coated member of the Leicestershire staff - a general factotum with a half-hearted moustache, portly in form, but several decades younger than the 'bouncers'. He spent some while discussing arrangements with an administrator from the New Zealand A team, due to play Leicestershire the next day, but also gave out information to a variety of enquiries from spectators, conveyed with a minimum of fuss - indeed often in monosyllables. For instance, a member asked why DeFreitas was on the pitch but not bowling. The reply was: "Groin."

Another (lady) member approached to ask if he knew which club it was that one of the umpires (Cowley) used to play for: "Hampshire."

The other umpire for this match, David Constant, was an entertainment in himself. Returning to his station at square leg after replacing the bails, he stopped, leapt high into the air, and twirled round 180 degrees, more like a member of the Bolshoi Ballet than a 59-year-old umpire. He responded to a universal, clamorous appeal off Kumble with a "not out" dramatic in voice and gesture. He sent a long, quizzical look in the direction of DeFreitas, who had playfully lobbed the ball near his back from third man, with a belated cry of "Connie".

Just as it seemed that Cassar and Krikken would hold out until the lunch interval Wells brought himself on, and persuaded Cassar to pull him high into the air in the mid-wicket region. Such was the ball's elevation that the two nearest fielders had time for unruffled negotiation as to who would catch it. Habib, elected, pouched it comfortably. Almost immediately Cork was lbw to the same bowler and Derbyshire - at 194 for 8 - were out of the game. In front of the pavilion Lewis became over excited, several times shouting out, obscurely: "Stand and deliver".

After the interval, Krikken struck a few more blows. Kumble seemed out of sorts. He bowled for the whole of the session before lunch and half-an-hour after it without taking a wicket. Once he aborted a delivery during his run-up - a rare occurrence - and ran down the pitch still holding the ball, looking, in his sprightly way, like a spring lamb gambolling in a meadow. Chris Lewis had bowled sparingly, despite Daffy's indisposition, but it was he who finished things off. He knocked out Krikken's off stump as the batsman drove at a full delivery. Wells dropped an easy low chance in the slips off Ormond, but in Lewis's next over showed how it should be done by taking a much more difficult chance, diving full length. Derbyshire were all out for 223, leaving their opponents 47 to win.

Leicestershire opened with Maddy and Ward, and needed no other contributions. Though Maddy had recently been the man to dominate the early stages of Leicestershire innings, Ward completely dictated this time. He took boundaries straight, fine to long leg, and high over mid-wicket. He followed this by hoisting the ball to the short square-leg boundary - the shortest available on the day. It bounced on the roof of the covered stand where I was sitting, and hit the top of the ground's outside wall. Next ball an even more violent stroke roared towards square leg about two feet off the ground, like an Exocet missile. Umpire Constant, doing his last turn of the day, threw himself flat to the turf with remarkable agility and quickness of thought, then regained an upright position as though nothing had happened.

As Leicestershire chalked up their second victory of the season a few spectators, through their radios, showed some interest in the Test match, in

61

progress at Edgbaston. Someone reported that England were 25 for 4 in their second innings, on the way to an innings defeat. I had been at Edgbaston the day before, and was struck by the disparity between spectators at Grace Road and Edgbaston. Most of the former were knowledgeable and attentive. It was not like that at the Test, where the match seemed predominantly to be 'a day out' for the lads - lads mostly incapable of sitting still to watch the game. Their priority was to swallow large quantities of beer, and they queued in shifts to buy it from overcrowded bars, missing half-hour slabs of the cricket. There were picnic boxes, Mexican waves, and patriotic chants, but informed comment was at a premium. If anything they resembled - God forbid - a football crowd (at a time when English football fans had disgraced themselves at the European Championships in Belgium).

The money earned from these vast Test match crowds is indispensable for the health of the counties, but it was hard to spot parallels between the two groups of spectators; harder still to feel that county matches were the dormitory for Test match crowds. Of the two sets of spectators, I knew which I preferred.

Leicestershire first innings

TR Ward	lbw	b Munton	5	**Bowling**	**O**	**M**	**R**	**W**
DL Maddy	c Di Venuto	b Munton	22	Cork	23	5	61	0
*VJ Wells	lbw	b Cassar	11	Munton	25	9	69	2
BF Smith	c Dowman	b Cassar	3	Cassar	15	2	62	4
A Habib		b Dean	164	Aldred	12.5	2	53	0
IJ Sutcliffe	c Krikken	b Cassar	43	Dean	8.4	1	47	4
CC Lewis	c Krikken	b Cassar	0	Bailey	6	2	9	0
PAJ DeFreitas		b Dean	37					
+ND Burns	not out		0					
A Kumble	lbw	b Dean	0					
J Ormond	lbw	b Dean	0					
Extras			25					
Total	All Out		**310**					

Derbyshire first innings

SD Stubbings	c Ward	b Ormond	0	**Bowling**	**O**	**M**	**R**	**W**	
MP Dowman		b Ormond	1	Ormond	14.5	2	50	6	
MJ Di Venuto		b Kumble	26	DeFreitas	23	8	39	2	
SP Titchard	c Kumble	b DeFreitas	16	Kumble	12	5	21	2	
RJ Bailey		b Kumble	11	Lewis	4	1	7	0	
ME Cassar	c Ward	b Ormond	30	Wells	2	1	4	0	
+KM Krikken	c Lewis	b Ormond	24	Maddy	1	0	1	0	
*DG Cork	lbw	b Ormond	1						
P Aldred	c Ward	b DeFreitas	5						
TA Munton	not out		0						
KJ Dean	c Lewis	b Ormond	0						
Extras			19						
Total	**All Out**		**133**						

Derbyshire second innings

SD Stubbings		b Ormond	8	**Bowling**	**O**	**M**	**R**	**W**	
MP Dowman	c Sutcliffe	b Wells	28	Ormond	24	7	58	2	
MJ Di Venuto	c Lewis	b Wells	13	DeFreitas	2	0	3	0	
SP Titchard	c Kumble	b Ormond	38	Wells	21	6	58	4	
RJ Bailey	lbw	b Kumble	24	Lewis	15.1	3	33	2	
KJ Dean	c Ward	b Kumble	0	Kumble	40	17	58	2	
ME Cassar	c Habib	b Wells	40	Maddy	3	0	6	0	
+KM Krikken		b Lewis	27						
*DG Cork	lbw	b Wells	0						
P Aldred	c Wells	b Lewis	10						
TA Munton	not out		0						
Extras			35						
Total	**All Out**		**223**						

Leicestershire second innings

TR Ward	not out	34	**Bowling**	**O**	**M**	**R**	**W**	
DL Maddy	not out	11	Cork	3	0	13	0	
Extras		2	Munton	5	3	13	0	
Total	**0 wickets**	**47**	Cassar	3	0	19	0	

Leicestershire won by 10 wickets. Points: Leicestershire 18, Derbyshire 3

George Dawkes, former Leicestershire wicket-keeper, at the
Oakham School game. He is the only survivor of the last
first-class game at Oakham in 1938. (Photo: Sylvia Michael)

Packing up after the match at Oakham School.
(Photo: Sylvia Michael)

8. Leicestershire versus Surrey
Oakham School, 7 to 10 July

The 9.28am train from Leicester to Oakham was unusually crowded, with the habitual clientele of commuters swelled by a different breed - men in blazers or sports jackets, carrying hampers, and talking about the last time first class cricket was played at Oakham School, in the year 1938. The rolling countryside seen through Central Trains windows emphasised the rural nature of the location, scene of the only Leicestershire home match played outside Grace Road in the 2000 season. The mood in the train was cheerful, despite the cold wind outside and the pall of low cloud cover - the last thing the organisers wanted to see.

The school facilities are a mere five minutes walk up the road from the station. The ground is famous for the quality of its pitch, but accountants are concerned about other matters, and there was much interest in how the Leicestershire management's bold venture in bringing the match here would work out. As one entered the school, the playing area took the breath away, because of its large size and the billiard-table quality of the turf. The setting was a mixture of the attractive and the ordinary. At the 'town end', Oakham Church spire appeared to rise from the mundane architecture of the school swimming pool. At the far 'playing field' end, beyond the Carling bar lorry and the burger bar, several more acres of sprightly turf stretched away into the distance, fringed by stately trees.

At this stage of the day, the cold, glowering weather seemed disastrous, squeezing the sense of adventure out of the whole enterprise and highlighting the limitations of part-time cricket grounds. There was no snug refreshment building or bar to retire to for warming up. The hospitality and 'committee' tents for the privileged few looked unwelcoming. The swimming pool toilets, unaccountably closed for periods of the match, were reached through changing rooms, where young boys' clothing was strewn about. The public address system, warbling unintelligibly, might have come from the bottom of the pool itself, though things improved later in the day. What should have been a peaceful, rural scene was shattered, as most such occasions are, by an ever-present generator serving the mobile bar; its unremitting roar suggesting that a combine harvester was operating in the adjacent field.

Surrey had won the toss. With precedents as to the quality of the wicket in short supply, they played safe and batted. Mark Butcher and Ian Ward opened in cold, overcast conditions which gave little pleasure to players or spectators. Butcher, coming straight from an unbeaten score in the 90s the previous day, played as though a night's sleep had not intervened and, swiping at Ormond, was caught in the slips. Progress was funereal. The first shot worth more than a single occurred in the seventh over. Ormond at least was enjoying the cool weather, running in flat out, and soon had Ward out lbw. When Adam Hollioake was very deliberately plucked up from ground level by Chris Lewis at second slip, Surrey were 25 for 3, all to Ormond.

Alec Stewart and Graham Thorpe were out of the Surrey side because of a one-day international match against Zimbabwe, but plenty of good players remained. Nadeem Shahid was joined by Alistair Brown, who took a fruitless swipe at the first ball of an Ormond over (a bouncer), was beaten outside off stump by the next ball, just removed his bat in time from the fourth, but cut the fifth square for four to the hospitality tent. It was the first of a number of pre-lunch runs he struck square on both sides of the wicket. Shahid, only slightly overshadowed, also accumulated quickly. By lunch Surrey were 112 for 3, Brown having just reached his half-century. Leicestershire had bowled DeFreitas, Lewis, Wells, Kumble and Maddy, but none had matched Ormond's threat.

I walked around the ground during the lunch break, to keep warm. The atmosphere was distinctly different from a Grace Road occasion. Despite the conditions a good crowd had materialised, of varied provenance. On top of a generous helping of Grace Road regulars, scores of the cricketing 'great and good' had turned up 'for the occasion', and were being punished by the cold for wearing blazers and ties. Many Surrey supporters were there, distinguishable by their accents. On top of this social panorama were the locals, notably people connected with the school; these included large groups of young children congregated at two corners of the pitch, where they played with computer games and sketch pads, and occasionally threw plastic bags onto the outfield. Presumably for their benefit, a man in a Mickey Mouse costume lurked behind one of the sightscreens, once tripping over a corner of the covers. It was odd to see Lewis, the cheerleader, out of his natural habitat at Grace Road. He lurked behind the sightscreen at the town end, wearing a colourful red and yellow windcheater with matching red cap. I had not yet seen him in the same outfit twice.

After lunch the sun came out; the appearance of the ground changed, and so did the play. DeFreitas had both Shahid and the younger Hollioake caught, rendering Surrey 125 for 5. Then Batty joined Brown, and together they added over 50 for the sixth wicket. From the beginning of his innings Brown was in do-no-wrong mood. While other Surrey batsmen scraped and prodded, he played all the bowlers with supreme confidence. His reputation as a one-day tonker of the ball was belied as he carefully constructed an innings, impressive in shot selection, and masterly in judgement of length. He was unfussy in his stance at the wicket, standing very still, and moving neither forward nor back until the moment of contact, when he put a raised bat very precisely to ball. The positive approach was typified by his running between wickets: whoever the partner, Brown was usually halfway down the pitch for a second or third run while his companion was still turning; when 'threes' or 'fours' were on the card, the partner was close to being lapped.

Brown reached 99 with a boundary through the covers, and went to 100 with almost his only false shot - an edge to long leg. It included 12 fours and came off only 129 balls, and was made out of a total of 173, though he came in at third wicket down. Despite the centurion's contribution, Surrey's total remained modest, and when Lewis snapped up Batty in the gully and then had Bicknell caught at the wicket, they were 190 for 7.

I was sitting next to a man who had been present at that 1938 first class match, the last to be played at Oakham. Here was a true cricket fan, of the sort who underpin the whole game, and he had passed the enthusiasm on to both son and daughter, who were sitting beside him. It was sadly clear, from his laboured wheezing, that the man was no longer in good health, and his brain was finding difficulty with numbers - so that his son frequently put him right on the length of a partnership or the number of overs left in the day. He spoke rarely, and then with an economy that I at first mistook for moroseness, but his brief comments revealed a keen interest in details of the play: "not using Kumble much, are they?"; "quite a tall chap, Bicknell"; "first no-ball of the day, I think"; "must be Stevens at long leg"; and so on. When the son asked how many grounds he had watched Leicester play on, his father totted up eight - a total redolent of another age. At Ashby, he said, "they used to stop play when the trains went by". It was a pleasure to sit silently beside this man and eavesdrop on his experience. I hope I am wrong in surmising that he does not have too many future summers of cricket left; but right in thinking that his son will still be watching forty years hence, perhaps with his son beside him.

Tea was taken with Surrey on 213 for 7; Brown was on 115 and Tudor on 7. Alex Tudor is perhaps a more familiar figure to England supporters as a batsman than a bowler, because of his famous 99 not out in a Test match, when he was deprived of his century by what many saw as Graham Thorpe's selfishness at the other end. In the flesh his height, accentuated by a slim build, made Tudor appear six inches tall than anyone else on the pitch. Playing a forward defensive stroke, he seemed to uncoil like a boa constrictor, his left leg advancing yards down the pitch, while his right remained anchored to the crease.

It seemed odd to say it, since the player already had 115 runs to his credit, but after tea Brown really got going. He reached 150 during an over from DeFreitas, in which he struck two straight fours, a boundary to square leg, and a couple of twos to the same position. Ten more off an over from Kumble seemed mild in comparison. When the 100 partnership came, Tudor had made a mere 11 of them.

By now the sun was warming a marvellous summer evening. A crowd of 1,500 people sat in shirt sleeves. The tall trees cast their shadows across the pitch, rooks cawed, and a couple of sparrows gambolled on a green baize outfield so smooth that their feet barely sank below the grass. A Surrey supporter, beer in hand, remarked to his companion: "This is as good as it gets, isn't it?"

As Brown neared his double century the scoring rate slowed. Kumble at last caused some circumspection, and Lewis bowled a long, tight spell. Tudor was dropped in the covers then, lashing out, marvellously caught by Maddy, over his shoulder diving backwards at mid-wicket. Brown reached 200, with 24 fours and a six. Amazingly, with a double centurion on their card, the Surrey total was still within Leicestershire's reach. Play closed on 334 for 8, with Brown's 211 not out comprising 63 per cent of the total. Right at the end of the day he was dropped by Burns, diving full length to his left, but at that stage of the innings it did not seem to matter too much.

Second day

The weather on the second day was an improvement on the first: cloudy and sunny in turns, but not very cold. Leicestershire were operating with the second new ball, but already had the field back for Brown, and concentrated on getting Ian Salisbury out. He was in no mood to oblige, striking a couple of boundaries and an all-run four. Play was held up by a man ascending a ladder onto the flat roof of the swimming pool, and then again, interminably, by fidgetings with the sightscreen. Finally Salisbury was out, caught by a diving Maddy at gully. Surrey were 364 for 9. The Surrey last man came out, and Leicestershire supporters prepared to see their team bat.

It was not to happen for quite a while. Brown continued to score in singles, partly perhaps through tiredness, but mainly because Leicestershire put five men on the boundary for him. From the start of his innings, Saqlain Mushtaq in no way resembled a number 11 batsman. After Wells had bowled him two bouncers in a row, Saqlain advanced yards down the pitch and crashed the ball to square leg, where it savaged a plastic chair. He followed this with two resplendent boundaries through the covers, possibly taking extra pleasure from the second of these shots off Kumble, an Indian leg spinner. Another charge down the pitch brought an enormous hit to long on, the ball bouncing just inside the rope. It was too much for one Saqlain supporter, who had obviously managed to get hold of the public address microphone; an announcement in a strong Pakistani accent said: "Well played, Saqqy. Well done, Saqqy boy", before being abruptly terminated.

Vince Wells's thoughts at this stage could only be guessed at. Instead of getting Surrey out for 200 - which could easily have happened - he was watching his opponents pass the 400 mark, still going strongly. Leicestershire had fought hard, but once a vehicle starts running away down hill, it gathers speed fast. At 266, Brown passed his previous highest score. DeFreitas was twice no-balled in an over for an excess of high-pitched deliveries. The crowd sat, unbelieving, as the last wicket partnership mounted. Cheerleader Lewis, for no apparent reason, sang a chorus of *"We shall not be moved"* over and over again.

Lunch was taken at 455 for 9, but the sight of Adam Hollioake conducting a training session in the nets at the end of the interval suggested that there was to be no declaration. Saqlain reached his 50 to wild enthusiasm from his personal fan club, leaping and whirling on the long-on boundary. At 460 for 9 Brown, clearly tiring, gave an easy return catch to James Ormond, who juggled, dropped it, then let his head sink into the turf in despair. The 100 partnership went by. Brown moved into the 290s with a cover drive off Wells, taking the overall score past 500.

Leicestershire's frustration gave way to resignation; they would allow Brown to reach his triple century and then hope for a declaration. But cricket has a way of tearing up the script. With the score on 505, Wells deceived Saqlain and bowled him for 66. Brown was left on 295 not out. He gave Saqlain a pat on the back of the head as they walked off, to show there were no hard feelings. After all, had it not been for 'Saqqy', Brown would not have advanced his score much beyond 200.

The Leicestershire innings began mid-afternoon with some very dark clouds overhead. No-one knew quite what to expect from the pitch. One spectator forecast at the start of the second day that the match would "end up a draw", while another reckoned it would be "all over in two-and-a-half days". Leicestershire's only real game plan was to bat as long as possible, accumulate bonus points, and deprive their rivals Surrey of points.

But a familiar bind, psychological and practical, affects teams which have conceded a vast first innings score: they brood on opportunities missed, while the opposition is buoyed up, and can afford the luxury of super-aggressive field settings. The Surrey field certainly looked highly concentrated, with three slips, point, gully and forward short-leg clustered round the bat. The vultures were soon in action, too. Sutcliffe was taken at slip off Tudor from an aggressive stroke played far too early in the innings. Maddy followed, caught off Martin Bicknell by Adam Hollioake at third slip, immediately after Holioake had moved to that position. It was 12 for 2.

Tudor and Bicknell were running in very fast, bending their backs, and getting impressive lift and movement from the pitch. But the next fall of wicket was self-inflicted by Leicestershire. Ben Smith struck the ball straight to mid-on, set off for a suicidal run, saw the stumps fly, and began a very slow, sad walk back to the pavilion. Habib came in and departed immediately, to Brown's second catch at slip, this time off Bicknell. It was now 27 for 4, with the Leicestershire innings in complete disarray. Lewis, behind the sightscreen, was incoherent with disappointment. People tried to console him, but he could not coax a response from choked vocal chords.

The procession continued. Stevens was out lbw to Tudor, playing no stroke. Chris Lewis, not for the first time in the season going back when he should have been forward, was lbw to Bicknell for a duck. On the stroke of tea Wells played a poor shot to a Tudor half-volley, and was caught at short extra cover. Tudor and Bicknell had taken three wickets apiece, and Leicestershire were 51 for 7, in reply to a score of 505. Ground staff at the school were already expressing concern that the pitch might be deemed unfit for a four-day match. But no logical explanations could justify the situation.

After tea, Surrey wheeled out their feared spin combination of Saqlain and Ian Salisbury, but Burns and DeFreitas put together a bit of a stand. Oakham appeared to reserve its best weather for the third session of play and, as on the first day, a large crowd enjoyed the warm evening sunshine.

Oakham School is an important dormitory for Leicestershire cricket talent, and the county had just set up a scholarship arrangement there. But the bedrock of Leicestershire support does not come from the independent school sector. I was sitting just in front of three young chaps in their mid-twenties, former pupils of Oakham school, almost clones of each other in their confident demeanours, designer hair styles, and expensive casual clothes. They had travelled in from job locations elsewhere (in a sales department, in a recruitment agency) to this reunion occasion at the old school. The cricket was mildly of interest. They kept half an eye on the play, calling out "shot" now and then in what seemed to be the right places. One of them had clearly been a big wheel in the Oakham team, and they had a friend who was a member of the England women's team. But cricket was merely the pretext for a social occasion. They were mainly interested in networking - where 'x' was working or what 'y' was doing. They would no doubt attend the occasional matches in future years, most probably in the hospitality tents. I saw them later in the evening, sitting in chairs that they had shifted into the narrow gangway alongside the pitch; they did not move when someone pointed out that they were blocking the only access route.

A stand between DeFreitas and Burns doubled Leicestershire's paltry total. Daffy, yet again, was his team's top scorer. In this mood he looked, like Saqlain before him, a class batsman, and a promotion in the batting order was surely overdue. He only succumbed when Saqlain got one to jump from the pitch, and he was caught by Adam Hollioake for 38. Just as the Surrey fast bowlers had overshadowed Leicestershire's, Saqlain's sideways movement was getting more out of the pitch than Kumble's top-spin. The spin made one defensive stroke from DeFreitas scuttle around the gully area like a drunken cockroach, yielding a run to the fielders' confusion.

Leicestershire ended the day on 134 for 9. I had to leave immediately after the fall of DeFreitas, to take advantage of the somewhat eccentric train service from Oakham station. On the platform, two middle-aged, working class Leicestershire supporters glumly awaited the same train. The wife had only just heard of DeFreitas's dismissal: "DeFreitas is out too, is 'e." She groaned in dismay. " 'Ow many did 'e get?"

71

Her husband, feeling that his own inattention was the cause of Leicestershire losing another wicket (a remarkably common, if absurd phenomenon), was reproving himself bitterly. "I was talkin' to old Jack, an' as soon as I said 'I'm goin' now', 'e was out." He shook his head miserably. "I wish I'd stayed now."

They cared. Their whole-hearted reaction seemed in stark contrast to the casual, half-attention of that other group, the school's former pupils.

Third day

On Sundays there was no train service to Oakham until after lunch, so I arrived for the third day's play at 2pm. I had visions of a Leicestershire recovery, perhaps with Habib on 70 not out, but at the ground found a scene of desolation - in two senses. The high cloud cover had given way to a sheet of low rain cloud, already unloading onto the pitch in a way that would clearly prevent play for some considerable time. And the scoreboard showed Leicestershire 42 for 4, with Maddy, Sutcliffe, Wells and Habib already out in the second innings follow-on. It only remained to be seen whether the weather would permit Surrey to bowl out Leicestershire a second time.

I stood under the trees to eat a couple of sandwiches, and watched the rain splash into a cup of tea bought from the Burger Grill stall. A knot of spectators had gathered under the same trees and were keeping their spirits up, and a few people stayed in their seats under striped brollies, but not surprisingly there was a remorseless drift of people out of the ground - several small boys among them, stolid disappointment in their faces. Here was the downside of watching cricket.

After a couple of hours the weather relented. The rain stopped and the sky cleared. The small boys reappeared and began kicking balls about on the outfield, soon joined by a few of the Surrey players. The ground, an astonishingly quick dryer, seemed none the worse for wear, and play began at 4pm, after an early tea, with 42 overs left until close of play. Bicknell's pounding feet, on his run-in, raised a series of small splashes, but of course Surrey were desperately keen to play.

Smith and Stevens were batting. The field setting was such that any aggressive shot was likely to score, and Smith struck a couple of boundaries before edging Bicknell, for Brown to take his third slip catch of the match. Chris Lewis replaced him and eked out 24 runs, though always looking impermanent. He was caught at the wicket off Ben Hollioake, bowling in place of Tudor who had dropped out with an injury (shades of Lewis himself). Leicestershire were 118 for 6.

If there was a plus factor in this sorry performance, it was the batting of Darren Stevens. Once again Stevens's good eye and sense of adventure, if not always his footwork, led him to a series of elegant boundaries. We saw drives, straight and through the covers, and cuts, late and square. Once he drove Salisbury through mid-wicket with a turn of the wrists that brought to mind India's Azharuddin, one of the few purveyors of this stroke in world cricket. Then, when he had reached 68 and cheered the dejected Leicestershire supporters, Stevens padded up to Saqlain and was bowled. Another promising, but ultimately unfulfilled Stevens innings had ended early; his reluctance to leave the crease showed the missed opportunity.

Not that playing the Surrey spinners was an easy option. Saqlain and Salisbury were bowling in tandem now, as they did at the end of most matches involving Surrey. Salisbury looked a leaner, more hungry bowler than the long-haired, pudgy figure tried out several times by England. In this match it was Saqlain, not content with his 66 not out, who took the wickets. Sidling in off half a dozen innocent steps, he tortured one batsman after another into indecision. DeFreitas (yet again) and Burns put on 30 runs together while the spinners wheeled away, and fielders clustered ever closer to the crease. Brown bowled a single over to switch Saqlain and Salisbury round - given his fortunes in this game, it was surprising that he did not secure a hat-trick - and the change did the trick, leading to Burns being caught at the wicket off Saqlain. Leicestershire were now 182 for 8.

. The match was all but over, yet those hard-core spectators who had survived the rain break sat on, leaning forward in their seats, absorbed in the last rites. A no-ball from Saqlain raised a murmur of interest. A Surrey fielder crashing dangerously into a 'PPP Healthcare' hoarding provoked some ironic speculation.

Now just one matter remained to be resolved: could Surrey finish the match off on the third day? The weather forecast for the fourth day was appalling, so from Leicestershire's point of view holding out until stumps might deprive Surrey of the points - though it would also oblige the team to hang about in the pavilion rather than having a day off. At 182 for 8, six and a bit overs remained, but the clouds had suddenly closed in, threatening a premature end through rain or poor light.

The spinners continued to amble in menacingly. DeFreitas had lengthy repairs to a damaged finger, but would not leave the field. From the boundary, Kumble could hardly be seen through the press of surrounding fielders. To an enormous shout, he was caught by Adam Hollioake off his pad. Nine wickets down. Ormond came out as last man. Rain had begun to fall and the light was dreadful. With a stoppage imminent, Ormond was given lbw to Saqlain. Leicestershire, all out for 184, had lost by an innings and 178 runs. Saqlain took 5 for 35. The rejoicing Surrey fielders gathered in a huddle mid-pitch, but not for long; the rain came down fiercely, driving them into the pavilion, and flushing the remaining spectators out of the ground. The neon strip above the Burger Grill stall glowed like a Las Vegas casino sign.

Most other county games of the day were 'no play, rain' draws, and the 20 points gained by Surrey took them to the top of the table. In the appalling summer, wins had been very hard to come by, and no more than 25 points separated the top five teams. All the same Leicestershire, having fallen to fourth equal position, would be beginning to worry - not only about not winning the championship, but also about falling further. But that, after all, was the point of the new, two-division formation, which was beginning to make itself felt.

One element of the new system still needed attention. Leicestershire won three bonus points for conceding more than 500 runs in Surrey's first innings, and being bowled out twice for peanuts. Who said that you cannot get something for nothing?

Surrey first innings

MA Butcher	c Wells	b Ormond	0
IJ Ward	lbw	b Ormond	6
N Shahid	c Burns	b DeFreitas	37
*AJ Hollioake	c Lewis	b Ormond	4
AD Brown	not out		295
BC Hollioake	c Habib	b DeFreitas	2
+JN Batty	c Lewis	b Maddy	19
MP Bicknell	c Burns	b Lewis	5
AJ Tudor	c Maddy	b Wells	22
IDK Salisbury	c Maddy	b DeFreitas	12
Saqlain Mushtaq		b Wells	66
Extras			37
Total	All Out		**505**

Bowling	O	M	R	W
Ormond	34	4	92	3
DeFreitas	29	6	115	3
Kumble	35	5	101	0
Lewis	18	2	60	1
Wells	17.5	1	65	2
Maddy	15	2	59	1

Leicestershire first innings

DL Maddy	c AJ Hollioake	b Bicknell	10
IJ Sutcliffe	c Brown	b Tudor	1
*VJ Wells	c Saqlain Mushtaq	b Tudor	13
BF Smith	run out		3
A Habib	c Brown	b Bicknell	0
DI Stevens	lbw	b Tudor	6
CC Lewis	lbw	b Bicknell	3
PAJ DeFreitas	c AJ Hollioake	b Saqlain Mushtaq	38
+ND Burns	c AJ Hollioake	b Saqlain Mushtaq	30
A Kumble		b Salisbury	10
J Ormond	not out		5
Extras			24
Total	All Out		**143**

Bowling	O	M	R	W
Bicknell	11	3	41	3
Tudor	11	6	34	3
Salisbury	18	8	29	1
Saqlain Mushtaq	17.2	8	25	2

Leicestershire second innings

DL Maddy	c Batty	b Bicknell	0
IJ Sutcliffe	c Batty	b BC Hollioake	14
*VJ Wells		b Bicknell	9
BF Smith	c Brown	b Bicknell	20
A Habib	st Batty	b Saqlain Mushtaq	4
DI Stevens		b Saqlain Mushtaq	68
CC Lewis	c Batty	b BC Hollioake	24
PAJ DeFreitas	not out		25
+ND Burns	c Batty	b Saqlain Mushtaq	8
A Kumble	c AJ Hollioake	b Saqlain Mushtaq	0
J Ormond	lbw	b Saqlain Mushtaq	0
Extras			12
Total	All Out		**184**

Bowling	O	M	R	W
Bicknell	15	4	44	3
BC Hollioake	15	4	48	2
Salisbury	14	4	41	0
Saqlain Mushtaq	15	4	35	5
Brown	1	0	8	0

Surrey won by an innings and 178 runs. Points: Surrey 20, Leicestershire 3

Views of Grace Road:
Top: The Bennett end. Bottom: Bench seats and the tea room
(Photos: Peter David Lush)

9. Leicestershire versus Durham
Grace Road, 12 to 15 July

From the first moments of this match, the subject of 'the pitch' was on everyone's lips. The lady in charge of Grace Road's shop reported, on the morning of day one: "It's a dreadful pitch, apparently. They were going to move it this morning." She said the decision to use it was only made at the last minute. I thought that her obvious concern and sense of involvement were touching. Grace Road has a family atmosphere.

Dreadful or not, Leicestershire chose to bat on winning the toss. After recent innings they desperately needed a good start, but found themselves 19 for 3, and then 37 for 4. Poor Leicestershire starts are so common that they cannot all be put down to early life in the pitch, but today it was soon clear that variable bounce would be a problem. Wells, Maddy and Sutcliffe were quickly back in the pavilion. Habib looked like staying around, but then hung his bat outside off stump and was caught at the wicket. Low bounce was the main concern, but the occasional ball leapt from a length, giving batsmen the worst of both worlds. From one of these, Ben Smith got a nasty bang on the elbow, and needed several minutes to recover.

Durham's Steve Harmison, who would have proved a handful on this surface, was not playing, but the northern county had their usual nap hand of capable seamers. Melvyn Betts and Simon Brown opened the bowling. Betts, with a shortish, bustling run-up and slinging delivery was distinctly lively. Brown's approach to the wicket was more military. Durham's fielders, maniacally keen, saved numerous runs in the outfield, but the field placings seemed conservative; for instance Brown, with four wickets down cheaply, bowled to one slip. The opening bowlers were supplemented by Wood, Killeen and Collingwood. Collingwood may have been disconcerted by a comic first delivery, when he ran up, fell over, and failed to release the ball.

Darren Stevens came to the wicket oblivious, as ever, of any crisis. Some trademark flicks to fine leg, and drives straight and past cover, took him up to Smith's score, and Leicestershire past 50. Two more fours followed, one of them his astonishing whipped stroke to the square leg boundary. Ben Smith responded with a high, pulled boundary and a four through the covers. At lunch Leicestershire were 84 for 4, with Smith on 32 and Stevens 28.

A woman in her sixties, walking past me with the aid of two sticks, remarked to her husband "I wonder if it's still like a bordello in there".

Overheard snatches of conversation can be tantalising. What was she referring to - the lady's toilets, the refreshment room, the ice-cream parlour?

Lunchtime visions of the definitive Stevens innings soon faded. Delightful drives straight and to square-leg were followed, two balls later, by a tame aerial push to point. Stevens returned furiously to the pavilion, head down, red-faced. He was replaced by DeFreitas, who had at last been given a position in the order that his season's batting form demanded.

Like most games these days, test or county, this one was disfigured by numerous delays. There were several stops to examine the ball and, after lunch, to change it. A lengthy intercession was needed to clear a whole group of schoolchildren off the roof of the Bennett building, where they were directly in the line of the batsman. Play was held up by an announcer relaying lunchtime scores, until an unceremonious "Shuddup" from the Durham captain shut him off in full flow. When DeFreitas was caught at slip off Killeen, Burns took an age to replace him, and had both umpires peering towards the pavilion, perhaps contemplating a rare decision of timed out.

Umpire David Shepherd does not seek stardom, but his personality and rare ability make him, in the public's eye, more famous than many of the players. With his dumpling figure he was unlikely to emulate David Constant's twirling and diving in Leicestershire's recent match with Derbyshire, but Shepherd's more sober antics still took the eye. Just after Burns came out he crossed from the umpire's square-leg position for the right hander to that for the left hander, and paused playfully between batsman and wicket as the player took guard from his fellow umpire; Shepherd's ample frame obscured the wicket, and no doubt half the pavilion as well.

He may have been late arriving, but Burns played a valuable role in the middle order, settling down to crease occupation while Ben Smith tried to bolster Leicestershire's inadequate score. No-one would have guessed, from seeing his innings here, that Smith had failed to pass 50 in any previous innings this season. His pre-lunch session at the wicket had yielded few scoring strokes, but the intense period of preparation now began to pay off. Most of Smith's strokes were in the off-side area between square and cover. He struck Collingwood on the up through the covers, and followed this with a vicious square cut, executed in one quick, fierce movement. Two more square cuts off Killeen took him past 50 for the first time that year.

Smith continued to flourish, with a rare force on the on-side, and a drive through the covers on one knee. The Leicestershire score inched towards respectability. With the total on 162 Burns was caught by Katich at first slip off Wood, from one of the occasional balls that bounced. The stand had been worth an invaluable 52 runs.

Anil Kumble joined Smith shortly before tea. Throughout the season the second half of Leicestershire's batting order had reflected reputation rather than performance. Kumble had scored more than 1,000 runs for India and had a top test score of 88, but he was bottom of Leicestershire's batting table with an average of 4. Smith needed and deserved his support now, but did not get it. Kumble stopped to tie up his boot lace after one ball at the crease (not exactly a sign of meticulous advance preparation), then tried an extravagant stroke and was caught at point. At tea Leicestershire were 179 for 8, with Smith on 83.

Cricket offers a microcosm of the British class structure, still very much alive. At the interval a white-coated attendant ushered a truly colossal motor car out of the Grace Road gates, silver trimmings on the hood, pennant flying - the ultimate status symbol.

"Car an'alf, that is," the attendant said, as we watched the monster glide away. "Who's in it?" "Some judge."

After tea James Ormond buckled down to stay with Smith. Smith hooked Killeen to fine leg, and Ormond snicked a boundary, but with the score at 197 three successive maidens went by. This was a sensible, measured response to good bowling; no-one could complain about Smith's stroke-play, but patience was the virtue which had provided the foundation of the Leicestershire innings. At last he cover drove for four to bring up his county's 200, and on-drove to reach his own century. He had faced 239 balls and scored nine boundaries.

The intense contest, under a grey sky and in cold weather conditions, was fought out in abnormally quiet conditions at Grace Road, so much so that the shouts of fielders were all audible. Two Durham fielders, grazing in the leg-side outfield, heard the hyena laugh of Lewis, the cheer-leader, echoing from the pavilion area and glanced at each other uncertainly, like gazelles fearful of predatory attack.

John Wood was listed as Durham's twelfth man on the scorecard but had found himself in the team and had already taken three wickets. His powerful deliveries, propelled by a burly frame, were unpredictable and dangerous on this wicket. When the stand between Smith and Ormond had reached 49, Leicestershire's score stood at 222, and Smith's individual score 111. The double helping of "Nelson" drew frantic foot-lifting from umpire Shepherd, but not enough to stave off the fall of wickets. Ormond was bowled playing forward to Wood, and Boswell fell next ball. Wood finished with figures of 5 for 60.

Second day

Durham started the second day on 8 without loss, chasing Leicestershire's first innings score of 222. Speculation in the stands was rife. Was 222 a decent total on this wicket? What did the frequent references to "this wicket" imply? Was the early fall of wickets the result of a poor surface, or of Leicestershire batting inadequacies? The most disconcerting feature was a tendency, on a wicket of generally low bounce, for the odd ball to fly. Rumour was fuelled by the presence at Grace Road of Phil Sharpe, the ECB pitch liaison officer, and the recent deduction of 8 championship points from Middlesex for a poor pitch at Southgate (though the points were later restored on appeal).

There was also gossip about the make-up of the Leicestershire team. Chris Lewis had been dropped. Jonathan Dakin had scarcely played since the first few games of the season but had a batting average - posted on the ground noticeboard - of 93. There had been no convincing explanation for the continued omission of this talented and extravagant player.

Durham's side is often criticised for its lack of quality batsmen, but the morning's play belonged to them. Though Daley quickly fell, lbw to DeFreitas, Simon Katich and Jonathan Lewis began building a stand. Lewis, an unrepentant stroke player, began with a flurry of cuts and drives. Ominously for Leicestershire, Katich, easily Durham's best batsman, was constructing his defences for a substantial innings. The pair took the total to 50, though Katich scarcely disturbed the scorers. Kumble came on from the Bennett end early, at 11.50am, but Katich immediately hammered his first ball to the square leg boundary. The Indian seemed out of sorts.

Then came a contentious incident likely to have a big bearing on the match. Katich cut Kumble fiercely and set off for a run, but Ben Smith at slip made a fine stop and flicked it back to the wicketkeeper, who took off the bails. Umpire Shepherd, standing at square leg, immediately gave the

Australian out, to great Leicestershire celebration. But umpire Harris had noticed something amiss (probably, though it was never clear, that the bails had been disturbed before Burns had the ball in his hands). The umpires conferred, and Shepherd reversed his decision. Despite the crucial importance of Katich's wicket, Leicestershire did not demur. It was a good example of umpires working in tandem, and also of the value of players having confidence in officials.

Soon after this Lewis was bowled by Wells for 33, caught between going forward and back. Collingwood's arrival was the signal for Katich to let loose. He twice struck Kumble to the mid-wicket boundary, gave Maddy the same treatment, and hooked Ormond for another four. At lunch he had taken his score to 40, almost all of them struck on the leg side. Durham were 107 for 2, and very few balls had beaten the bat. Spectators shook their heads and referred back to the significance of the run-out incident. Several predicted a Durham total in the region of 300.

The change in fortunes after the break can be partially but not entirely explained. Ormond had Collingwood lbw for 22 immediately after play resumed, but the crucial wicket was that of Katich. Ormond intelligently kept the ball clear of the Australian's leg-side strokes, and got one to leap from a length, for Wells to take the catch at first slip. The fielders' joyful reception of this wicket betrayed its importance, and was no less sweet for being the second celebration of Katich's dismissal. When the young player, Ali, was lbw to the second Ormond delivery he received, Durham were suddenly 120 for 5.

Another reason for the turnaround was that Kumble changed ends, and shifted his line from leg to middle stump. He looked a completely different bowler. It is usually fatal to play back to the Indian's fizzing top-spin, but there is something about Kumble's trajectory which persuades batsmen to do just that. He bowled Speak, who went neither forward nor back, then had Betts lbw to the second strong appeal in the same over. The next victim was Speight, suicidally cutting at a ball of almost full length. Killeen came in, survived an lbw appeal off his first ball, was nearly caught off the second, and was leg before to the third. At the other end Ormond returned and sent Wood's middle stump back. Durham were all out for 171. Nine of their batsmen were bowled or lbw, normally a sign of low bounce - though only three Leicestershire wickets had fallen in this way.

After an early tea Leicestershire began their second innings, and busied themselves surrendering the advantage of a 51-run first innings lead. Sutcliffe (to a pair), Wells and Smith were all out cheaply. How rare it is for a first-innings centurion to make second innings runs. The scoreboard showed 25 for 3.

Brown had already taken two wickets when Habib flashed at him, sending the ball high over where third slip would have been. Then the reconstruction began. Habib and Maddy played themselves in and began cautiously to try some strokes. Durham circulated their five seam bowlers. Between them they bowled an excellent length, permitting very few cut or pull shots. Their fielding was as tenacious as ever, but at 55 for 3 Habib was badly dropped off a waist-high chance at second slip. At 74 he was dropped again, when a chance flew unhindered between first and second slips.

The score had reached 81 when the umpires consulted about the light. It was 6.30pm and four lights showed on the 'warning' panel. But play continued, and Maddy and Habib struck a flurry of boundaries, taking the overnight score to 98. Not for the first time it raised the puzzle as to why so many batsmen do 'take the light' and stop play, when they are well set and bowlers are tired.

Third day

Leicestershire began the third day's play 151 runs ahead of Durham, with seven wickets standing. The feeling among many observers was that another 100 runs would give them an excellent chance of victory.

A smallish crowd had turned out to watch. The windy, cold day, with heavy cloud cover, was one for enthusiasts only.

"Bloomin' cold," said a pensioner to a friend arriving at the ground. "Cold! You want some blood in yer alcohol stream."

Melvyn Betts had limped off the field, so Durham were down to four seamers plus the occasional spin of Katich. Wood bowled with three slips, for the first time in the match, and one wondered whether the attacking fields had come too late. Maddy and Habib continued their stand of the previous evening and, though beaten occasionally outside off stump, both took their scores to 50. When their partnership was worth exactly 100, Habib was caught off Brown at deep mid-off, from a low, skimming drive. The pair had rescued their team from a parlous early passage of play, and possibly set up a victory.

Simon Katich's spin was bowled from a run-up of four paces walking, two trotting. Darren Stevens faced him, coming in fourth wicket down, and missed a violent sweep at his first ball. He struck the second through the covers off a half-volley, and swept again at the third, skying the ball to mid-wicket, where it fell just short of the fielder running in from square leg. Another quiet Stevens opening.

Batting was still not easy, and Maddy was twice beaten by extra bounce from Simon Brown - the best of Durham's bowlers in the second innings. On the second occasion the ball fell to earth neatly between retreating slips and advancing third man. Despite the alarms he continued to score rapidly. Stevens's brief but merry appearance ended when he was caught behind down the leg side for 19. Shortly afterwards, Maddy pushed Killeen off his legs to short mid-wicket, where he was taken for 77. Leicestershire, at 181 for 6, were 232 runs ahead.

DeFreitas and Burns turned the screw on Durham with a stand of more than 40. Durham, with attacking field settings, retrieved the ball from the outfield with intensity, and early in his innings subjected Burns (batting with a dodgy finger, damaged at Oakham) to a torrid over which included four balls above waist height. But the match was slipping away. Just before lunch Daffy struck an enormous six to square leg. Collingwood, coming on for a new spell, emulated his slapstick initial delivery in the first innings with another circus act, bouncing his practice ball high over the fielder, whence it ran down to the sightscreen.

· After the break Leicestershire's innings subsided to some magnificent catching. DeFreitas tried to hit Katich for another six, but Speak ran back full pelt from mid-wicket and dived to take the ball falling over his shoulder. If this were not enough Kumble, again hitting out before he was set, was taken by Collingwood, diving at gully. Immediately Ormond was brilliantly caught by Katich, hurling himself full length at slip. The trio of catches was itself worth the price of admission. If Durham's batting matched their fielding, the team would be on top of the championship table.

By the time Boswell was last out, Leicestershire had reached 259, and secured a lead of 309. Simon Brown got in among the tail, and deservedly registered figures of 5 for 70.

Leicestershire began their final onslaught against Durham's batting just after 3pm, with Ormond bowling to three slips, a gully and a forward short leg. If Durham were to stand any chance of making the stiff total they needed a good start, but in no time Lewis was bowled by Ormond playing forward. Sutcliffe then took a reaction catch at forward short leg, off the second attempt, to dismiss Daley off DeFreitas. And the young Ali was out lbw to Ormond on the back foot, to a ball which kept low. Durham, at 19 for 3, were already on the slide.

Collingwood came to the wicket to join Katich, who bent to scrape the crease area free of loose dirt with a horizontal bat - an unusual sight. Ormond, really enjoying himself in this match, bowled for 90 minutes before tea. He powered in from the Bennett end and, directing a high proportion of his deliveries at the wicket, was rewarded by another clatter of stumps as Collingwood went only half forward to him. Batsmen were being defeated by good line and length, high speed, and low bounce.

Anil Kumble came on at the pavilion end, where he had done the damage in the first innings. Katich hit a tiring Ormond for two boundaries but, just before tea, a Kumble delivery leapt from a length, giving Sutcliffe an easy catch at forward short leg. The players went off. At tea, only a madman would have put money on a Durham victory.

The tea interval was a time for getting warm - in the bar, the refreshment room, or anywhere else out of the weather. In the shop, unnaturally crowded, a man murmured to an acquaintance: "I've come in 'ere for some warmin'". The lady in charge of the shop overheard him, and immediately retaliated: "We charge for warming, sir". No-one was fooled by her stern expression, which failed to conceal a kind heart; she was soon helping some "young gentlemen" to identify illegible autographs which they had collected from players at random. I bought a cup of tea in the refreshment room and sat next to a couple permanently installed there, with five thermos flasks set out on the floor among their equipment (and no thought of buying tea to pay for the roof over their head). "'Ave you bin out?" they asked an acquaintance, as if this was an act of folly, like leaving your tent at the South Pole.

Off his first ball after tea, and the last ball of the over, Kumble had Speight caught by Maddy at forward short leg. When the Indian began his next over, a field of three short legs, two slips and a leg slip seemed slightly over the top, until it dawned that another wicket would bring an unusual hat-trick - three balls separated by the tea interval and an over break. It was not to be, though Kumble soon persuaded yet another Durham batsman (Speak) to play back to him, and pay the penalty.

From the hopeless situation of 60 for 7, Wood and Betts - who was batting with a runner - constructed a small stand. Boswell had them playing and missing several times outside off stump, but could not adjust his radar onto the wicket. Ormond was brought back and, irresistible, bowled Wood in the first over of his new spell. The stand of 30 had taken the score to 93.

The end was nigh. Maddy took a wonderful catch at forward short leg, diving full length and clutching the ball inches off the ground to dismiss Betts off Kumble - the fourth catch from this position in the Durham second innings. Ormond provided a spectacular finish by yorking Killeen; the batsman plunged over forwards in his attempt to get his feet out of the way. Durham's sad total of 93 included 20 extras (and too many no-balls). Ormond had 5 for 34, and Kumble 4 for 23.

Why did Leicestershire beat Durham in this match? Because they were playing at home? Because they won the toss and had the best of the pitch (or less of the worst of it)? Because in Ormond and Kumble they had the two bowlers who could best take advantage of the conditions? Because they set more aggressive field placings? Or because their batsmen buckled down better to building an innings on a pitch of variable bounce?

The main complaint against the surface was one of low bounce, a feature which is generally thought to lead to more batsmen that usual being bowled and given lbw. In the match as a whole, Leicestershire batsmen suffered five dismissals in these categories, whereas Durham batsmen registered 15. This was an extraordinary statistic.

· The final word on the pitch came from umpire Shepherd. As the match ended, and the players came off the field, Shepherd was besieged by young autograph hunters, seeking to add England's most famous umpire to their list of monikers. He rolled on gently through the scrimmage, signing as he went. An adult spectator approached and asked: "What was the pitch like?" Shepherd went on signing, head down, and for a moment it seemed he would not respond. Then it came, as considered as his umpiring decisions: "It's not the best I've seen," he said in his soft, west country accent. "But it wasn't the worst."

Leicestershire first innings

DL Maddy	c Speight	b Brown	0
IJ Sutcliffe		b Betts	0
*VJ Wells	lbw	b Betts	12
BF Smith	not out		111
A Habib	c Speight	b Wood	9
DI Stevens	c Daley	b Wood	40
PAJ DeFreitas	c Katich	b Killeen	10
+ND Burns	c Katich	b Wood	10
A Kumble	c Daley	b Collingwood	3
J Ormond		b Wood	14
SAJ Boswell	c Speight	b Wood	0
Extras			13
Total	All Out		**222**

Bowling	O	M	R	W
Brown	21	7	41	1
Betts	23	7	40	2
Killeen	15	7	34	1
Wood	21.4	4	60	5
Collingwood	10	2	24	1
Katich	4	0	14	0

Durham first innings

JJB Lewis		b Wells	33
JA Daley	lbw	b DeFreitas	4
SM Katich	c Wells	b Ormond	43
PD Collingwood	lbw	b Ormond	22
*NJ Speak		b Kumble	18
SM Ali	lbw	b Ormond	0
+MP Speight		b Kumble	18
MM Betts	lbw	b Kumble	0
J Wood		b Ormond	15
N Killeen	lbw	b Kumble	0
SJE Brown	not out		0
Extras			18
Total	All Out		**171**

Bowling	O	M	R	W
Ormond	22.1	5	44	4
Boswell	10	3	28	0
Kumble	14	4	32	4
Wells	7	0	21	1
DeFreitas	17	6	36	1
Maddy	1	0	4	0

Leicestershire second innings

DL Maddy	c Lewis	b Killeen	77
IJ Sutcliffe	lbw	b Betts	0
*VJ Wells	c Speight	b Brown	10
BF Smith	c Betts	b Brown	8
A Habib	c Wood	b Brown	52
DI Stevens	c Speight	b Wood	19
PAJ DeFreitas	c Speak	b Katich	36
+ND Burns	not out		36
A Kumble	c Collingwood	b Brown	1
J Ormond	c Katich	b Brown	0
SAJ Boswell		b Killeen	12
Extras			8
Total	All Out		**259**

Bowling	O	M	R	W
Brown	21	2	70	5
Betts	11	4	20	1
Wood	21	4	59	1
Killeen	12.4	3	51	2
Collingwood	6	2	15	0
Katich	14	1	36	1

Durham second innings

JJB Lewis		b Ormond	5
SM Ali	lbw	b Ormond	7
JA Daley	c Sutcliffe	b DeFreitas	7
SM Katich	c Sutcliffe	b Kumble	18
PD Collingwood		b Ormond	8
*NJ Speak		b Kumble	9
+MP Speight	c Maddy	b Kumble	0
MM Betts	c Maddy	b Kumble	9
J Wood		b Ormond	10
N Killeen		b Ormond	0
SJE Brown	not out		0
Extras			20
Total	All Out		**93**

Bowling	O	M	R	W
Ormond	11.1	0	34	5
DeFreitas	6	0	14	1
Kumble	10	5	23	4
Boswell	5	0	18	0

Leicestershire won by 217 runs.
Points: Leicestershire 16, Durham 3

10. Surrey versus Leicestershire
Guildford, 19 to 22 July

There was a certain symmetry about Leicestershire's two fixtures with Surrey in 2000. Leicestershire staged their match away from Grace Road, at Oakham, and Surrey put theirs away from its headquarters at The Oval, playing it at Guildford. The Leicestershire team travelled to Guildford badly needing to win. This was not just a matter of revenge for their drubbing at Oakham School. Points for a win were essential if they were to stand any chance of overhauling their southern rivals in the championship table, where Surrey were already 25 points ahead of them (and 16 and 17 points respectively clear of Lancashire and Yorkshire, in second and third places).

If Oakham School is one of the most bucolic part-time cricket venues, Guildford is one of the least. The ground borders the A322, and a continuous stream of heavy traffic grinds past from the ugly centre of the town, obliterating any sound of willow upon leather. One might as well play cricket by the M25. Adding to the noise, trains run past one end of the ground on a line raised to mid-tree level.

The playing area is narrow, and even with spectators sitting bang on the ropes on either side, square leg and point boundaries are decidedly short. Knee-room in the cramped temporary stands was reminiscent of economy class on a cheap airline. For once in this grey season the match was played in fierce, hot sunshine. There were places where the trees afforded transient shade, but most of the crowd boiled in the open. On a minor point, Guildford was bereft of its customary 'angel'; according to a spectator, it had been taken down to be gilded.

Leicestershire won the toss and chose to bat, on a pitch which - everyone said - would take spin in the later stages. The threat of Saqlain Mushtaq loomed large, following his demolition of Leicestershire at Oakham, not to mention his 11 wickets in Surrey's previous match against Yorkshire. Lewis and Dakin were still missing from the Leicestershire side, and Surrey's Stewart and Thorpe were on one-day Test duty for England.

Surrey opened the bowling with Martin Bicknell and Carl Greenidge (son of Gordon). Sutcliffe square cut and cover drove the latter for successive fours, to boundary ropes which seemed unnervingly close after some of the big playing areas I had visited during the season. Maddy played an ill-advised forcing stroke to Bicknell and was caught at the wicket. Undeterred,

Stevens cut at his second ball from Bicknell, and off his third gave the bowler the simplest of return catches.

A total of 26 for 2 was a familiar-sounding Leicestershire score, but for once it did not lead on to 30 for 3, and 40 for 4. Sutcliffe was playing his best innings of the summer, tenacious in defence, but also embracing periodic shots to the short boundaries. He was joined by a Ben Smith batting with great confidence after his century against Durham.

At 10 minutes past midday a long spell by Martin Bicknell ended, and Saqlain made his first appearance. This was earlier than most spinners are seen in a county match, but Surrey appear to cut short the picador stage of a contest and move quickly to the man designated to deliver the *coup de grâce* by sword. The Pakistani began with one forward short-leg, who was reinforced by a second after two balls - a little psychological ploy which Surrey enacted several times in the match. The two masked men crouched a couple of yards from the bat whenever Saqlain was bowling. The demon spinner caused no immediate alarms. Smith struck a short ball through the covers in his first over, and Sutcliffe pushed a full toss for four in the next.

At 12.30pm the ball was changed. Even in a manufacturing age characterised by built-in obsolescence it was astonishing that a ball could not last more than 90 minutes. A change of product for county cricket matches is surely overdue.

When the score was 60, Smith attempted to hook Ben Hollioake hard and high over square leg and on to the short boundary there. Greenidge, fielding in this position, leapt high to parry the ball above his head, and caught it as he plunged to earth. A triumphant roar from the crowd turned to disappointment as the ball was seen running loose, dislodged as Greenidge hit the deck. Smith was on 19 at the time, and the incident was significant; with Sutcliffe he took the score on to 80 by lunch.

Saqlain had already changed ends once, and Bicknell and Saqlain resumed after lunch in what sometimes seemed a two-man bowling attack. Bicknell was still bowling at 2.40pm, at which time he had kept one end busy during the periods from 11.00 to 12.10, 12.55 to 1.15, and 1.55 to 2.40. It was not as if he used an effortless run-in. He started only a few yards short of the sight-screens, sprinted in full tilt, and hurled down fast-medium deliveries with a grunt signifying maximum effort. An almost unnaturally upright stance, before and during delivery, emphasised the man's height of six feet four inches. At 2.40pm his effort and skill paid off again, as a fast delivery swinging away from Sutcliffe had the batsmen caught by Alistair Brown at second slip. Leicestershire were 95 for 3.

To appreciate Bicknell's efforts fully one needed to take into account the heavy, sultry weather, which had more than a few spectators nodding off after lunch. Still awake, and looking very fit, former Prime Minister, and Surrey president, John Major strolled along the ground's perimeter behind the dozers. In the numerous hospitality tents lunches continued. Men in suits guzzled and swilled, and brayed in House of Commons mode, mostly with their backs to the play. The tents were an attractive sight, with their colourful umbrellas over an array of small tables, but they took up most of the best viewing positions in the ground (especially those behind the bowler's arm), making them available to people not interested in cricket. You had to wonder why they could not guzzle somewhere else.

For his third spell Saqlain changed ends again, replacing Bicknell. Salisbury, his usual spinning partner, was playing but not bowling, because of a sore shoulder. For a while Saqlain and Ben Hol025ioake made no progress against a Smith/Habib partnership of 50, until those masked short legs were at last called into action - Habib giving the easiest of bat/pad catches. Still the floodgates did not open to the Pakistani spinner, as Wells supported Ben Smith in another sizeable partnership. Smith, after his escape to Greenidge, proceeded with utter certainty through the 80s, cutting and cover driving regular boundaries.

With the score one short of 200 Wells was given lbw to Bicknell, on for another spell. Smith forged on, cover driving Bicknell for a four and a two to reach his century just before tea - off 182 balls, with 15 fours. It was his second hundred in successive matches, following a poor start to the season.

After tea Hol025ioake had the fast man on yet again. You could have argued that Bicknell was being seriously over-bowled, but this was obviously not the view of the bowler himself, since he put more and more deliveries in the right areas. He got rid of Smith, and then Burns, caught in the slips and behind the wicket respectively, leaving Leicestershire 226 for 7. You felt Surrey were working a form of confidence trick: Saqlain was the red-hot property, bowling all day on a pitch expected to take spin, but a 31-year-old pace man was knocking them over every time his captain called him for a spell.

Leicestershire had advanced in this match through a series of 50-run partnerships, and the fourth of these now took root. DeFreitas, from whom 30 or 40 runs were now expected (and achieved) every match, was one of the partners; the other was Dominic Williamson, a medium-paced bowler playing his first championship match of the summer. They endured an eventful Bicknell over early on: DeFreitas nobly responded to Williamson's call for a no-hope single, made his ground, and levelled his bat handle like a machine gun at his partner; Daffy was then caught behind off a no-ball, and advanced yards down the pitch next ball to play defensively; and, off the last ball of the over, Williamson bashed Bicknell to the long-on boundary.

The partnership went well past 50 with Bicknell and Saqlain again in harness, and Adam Hollioake apparently on auto-pilot as captain. Williamson looked every inch a batsman. Leicestershire passed 250 at a rate of three an over. One extraordinary feature, for a slow bowler, was Saqlain's regular no-balling; I stopped counting after eight of them. Despite the spinner's presence at one end the over rate was funereal, and play continued well into the evening. At 6.20pm, Salisbury at last turned an arm, to ironic cheers, and immediately had Williamson badly dropped at slip. As the evening closed in, a curious lassitude appeared to envelop the Surrey players and spectators alike. At last, well past 7pm, Adam Hollioake ended the deadlock, having Williamson caught behind for 47, and for good measure catching DeFreitas off Saqlain. Leicestershire ended the day on 313 for 9.

Guildford is a difficult town for accommodation. There were 'house full' responses from all the town centre addresses in the tourist information brochure. I ended up taking a room in a suburban house a 45-minute walk from the ground, on a route offering a very occasional bus service. The landlady was a control freak. You had to abandon your shoes at the front door and go to your room memorising a barrage of instructions, only to find there a collage of further instructions - "Please do not..." - fixed to the walls. The woman's husband had a subdued appearance; when she served a cup of tea she not only told him he could have just one biscuit from a box of assorted, but also identified the biscuit he was to have.

Second day

The hot weather continued on the second day. Surrey polished off the Leicestershire innings, and Bicknell finished with figures of 7 for 72, off 28 overs. Saqlain had a mere two wickets off 39 overs, but conceded fewer than two-and-a-half runs per over. No-one else bowled more than 12 overs in support of them.

A wicket fell immediately at the start of the Surrey innings. Butcher had been in atrocious form and, as so often happens, this attracted bad luck; he was given out caught down the leg-side, to everyone's astonishment, especially his own.

This misfortune merely presaged an excellent stand between Nadeem Shahid and Ian Ward. Shahid is a dashing, elegant figure on the field. The previous day he had torn about the outfield completely unencumbered by the short-leg pads worn under the trousers. Today he played crisply from the start, from a very upright stance. Ward matched him boundary for boundary, being particularly strong square on both sides of the wicket. The pair had put on 93 at four an over - interrupted, unbelievably, by another ball change after 90 minutes - when Kumble was brought on for the traditional spinner's over before lunch; a very poor over it was too, yielding nine runs, until to the last ball of the six Shahid unaccountably pulled a long hop into the hands of mid-wicket.

The fierce scoring pace continued after lunch until Adam Hollioake, aiming for a six to the short boundary at square leg, was caught on the rope by DeFreitas off Ormond, and departed for 18. Leicestershire fielders would not have been reassured by seeing Alistair Brown come to the wicket, not long after his 295 struck against them at Oakham School. In fact Brown was in sober mood, partly perhaps because of the soporific heat after lunch, and partly because of Surrey's need for retrenchment, at 123 for 3. The scoring rate dropped during a very quiet period of play, interrupted by the odd single.

It was a time for talking to neighbours in the crowd. I was quickly becoming aware that these southern supporters were a very different lot from those encountered at grounds further north. True, there were plenty of Guildford people attending their one match of the year - "I only get my head together for cricket during this festival" - but also numerous spectators who watched a very great deal of cricket indeed, and in many different locations. A Middlesex supporter, to whom Middlesex fixtures were "sacrosanct in the calendar", pointed out that there were a lot of Middlesex members at Guildford because their team had no match that day. Another man, a former university lecturer on Soviet politics, was a member of eight clubs; he had customarily watched 90 days of cricket a year, but was "cutting down". He was a shaggy, rumbustious character, who much preferred four-day cricket to the one-day game. The latter was like "seeing Yehudi Menuhin busking outside the Albert Hall".

"Cricket travelling" seemed in part a function of the greater number of grounds within range of Londoners, and perhaps also of the larger wallets needed to support multiple club memberships and the considerable travelling expenses. Although the travellers usually watched one county more than the others, their affiliations were much weaker than those of, say, a Leicestershire fan; they turned out primarily to 'see some cricket' - rather than to see their side win. Most would probably have recoiled from a statement that they "loved the game" as being too florid, but watching it meant a great deal to them. And they were extremely well informed.

The sweltering afternoon, with its peaceful passage of play, belonged to Ward and Ormond. Ward built his innings with all the certainty of Ben Smith the previous day, driving through the covers and square. Kumble was expensive, and for quite a stretch of the afternoon there was the bizarre sight of Ormond - Leicestershire's quickest bowler - bowling off-breaks while a world-class spinner rested in the covers. Another oddity was that Ormond obliged Brown to retire hurt when a no-ball struck the Surrey player on the forearm, an unfortunate incident which certainly disturbed Surrey's rhythm. Not content with offering two types of bowling, Ormond made a couple of whole-hearted rolling stops on the boundary, hurling his 14-stone frame to the ground and throwing powerfully back to the wicketkeeper. In spinner mode, he took Ben Hollioake's wicket for 20, as Sutcliffe threw himself forward at short square-leg. Even so Surrey, at 198 for 4, seemed on top.

Kumble returned, seeming marginally keener to bowl, and had Batty caught with casual ease by Habib in the covers. He remained expensive, and his last over before tea disturbed the sleepy atmosphere of the afternoon: a no-ball was followed by four byes and a wide - a cocktail of extras - before the final, very short ball was struck for four to square leg. "It's quite exciting now!" said a lady unpacking a tea-time hamper.

After tea Ward went to his century, off 206 balls with 13 fours, and Surrey went well past the 250 mark. A Surrey supporter said: "I think we can get 400 today", and may have regretted it for, in one of cricket's sudden reversals of fortune, their dominance was rudely interrupted. Brown had returned to the crease, but was caught at the wicket off Ormond for 34. Bicknell followed immediately, lbw to the same bowler. Ward began to take risks: one aerial shot off DeFreitas cleared cover, but he tried it again and was easily caught by Habib. Saqlain charged down the wicket to Ormond and gave Habib his third catch. Greenidge fell lbw to Kumble. Surrey were all out for 288.

The similarities between the Leicestershire and Surrey first innings were extraordinary. Both had relied upon a centurion, with supporting roles from a few players (the second highest score being 47 in both cases). The bowling had been dominated in both innings by one performance - with Bicknell taking seven wickets and Ormond six. On more minor matters, both sides had been guilty of very slow over rates, and both had given away far too many extras - 53 in Surrey's case and 41 in Leicestershire's.

The match had lasted almost two days, but had yet to hint at its outcome. This was about to change. Leicestershire began their second innings at 6.15pm, with prospects of about an hour's play before them. They had a first-innings lead of 30, and would have been optimistic about their prospects of victory over the championship leaders if they could keep most of their wickets intact until the third day. The pitch was expected to take increasing amounts of spin, and Surrey had to bat last (although the threat of Saqlain in the Leicestershire innings could not be overlooked).

The innings began with the now familiar sight of Martin Bicknell charging in from the pavilion end. His first five deliveries were all wide of the off stump, and Darren Maddy let them go. The sixth knocked Maddy's middle stump back as he reached for a forward stroke. Bicknell had secured Maddy's wicket in all four of his season's innings against Surrey: for 10 and a duck at Oakham, and 3 and a duck at Guildford.

Bicknell's second over, to Sutcliffe, was more eventful: off the first ball Sutcliffe struck him to the square-leg boundary; from the second, he was dropped by Butcher at slip; the third was struck for two to mid-off, and the fourth knocked the batsman's leg stump clean out of the ground. The crowd's roar was positively gladiatorial. How uplifting it is for the fielding side to see stumps fly, not once but twice in quick succession.

Stevens came out to join Ben Smith. The Leicestershire batting order is a continuously moveable affair, with only Maddy at one and Habib at five inviolable. Smith edged Greenidge high over third slip for four, then dropped to one knee and struck him through the covers. Stevens, ever the dasher, took three fours off Bicknell. It was 7pm in the evening and the hospitality tents were virtually empty, no further glad-handing being on offer. Shadows from the trees bordering the ground reached across to fielders on the leg-side, and engulfed the square-leg umpire. Leicestershire were 31 for 2. The fielders' cries urged Bicknell to secure "one more" before close of play. Three slips and two gullies gathered behind the wicket.

Stevens, unable to help himself, drove at Bicknell and was caught at slip by Butcher, redeeming his earlier drop. Burns came out as night watchman, sundering the batting order even further. Bicknell, irresistible, swept him aside leg before. This brought out Habib, Leicestershire's key batsman, at 31 for 4. The man next to me had got up to go and put on his jacket and satchel, but stood undecided, unable to tear himself away. By now Bicknell's charging figure was invested with superhuman powers. Habib played defensively at him, nicked the ball, and was again taken by Butcher. Amid uproarious rejoicing from the crowd, Bicknell and all the slips charged spontaneously forward 20 yards to an area in front of the scoreboard, where they twirled and leapt about and cried hoarsely to each other, like a congregation of sea lions. Bicknell, at the end of his spell for the day, walked about in his elongated, almost robot-like manner, to be high-fived by every member of the Surrey side. His spell of seven overs had yielded 5 for 25.

It was 7.30pm. At the other end Ben Smith had survived because he was not facing Bicknell. In the last over of the day he padded up to an accurate Greenidge delivery - perhaps blinded by tears in his eyes - and was lbw. Leicestershire took an overnight score of 33 for 6 into the third day. If it had been a boxing match the referee would have stopped it there and then.

Third day

Despite the state of the match a reasonable crowd turned up to the third day's play. Guildford were charging full price for entrance - unlike Leicestershire who, faced with a very similar situation in a recent match against Derbyshire, had let people in free to the truncated day.

With all passion spent on the previous day, the atmosphere was one of awaiting the inevitable. Wells and DeFreitas put up some resistance, doubling the Leicestershire score in the first 20 minutes, and Wells even struck Bicknell flat-batted for six over point. After a few overs Bicknell again began to find his deadly range. A riotous shout for lbw against Wells was answered by umpire Holder raising an arm and whirling round to signal a no-ball. Timing is everything in an umpire's performance. Soon after this came a familiar snick, a clutch at slip, and a departing batsman - DeFreitas, falling to Butcher's third catch of the innings. Two balls later the same ritual led to Brown taking another slip catch from Wells. Kumble decided to depart in a different manner, advancing down the wicket to spoon Bicknell to Ben Hollioake at point. Finally Bicknell ended the innings as he had begun it, by knocking the stumps down dismissing Ormond for a duck. Leicestershire were all out for 87.

Every newspaper on the following morning drew attention to Bicknell's feat. He had added 9 for 47 to his first innings 7 for 72, and in the process notched up the best championship match return for more than 40 years, and the best ever for Surrey. A local lad, he also had the best ever bowling figures at the ground. He had bowled fast, with great endurance, to an excellent length, and swung the ball consistently away towards the slip cordon. He was "pleased", he said on radio that evening; he had "put the ball in the right place and they either edged it or missed it".

There were no surprises left. Ward, prospering again, and Butcher took Surrey's second-innings score to 53 at lunch. Even at this stage the Guildford management was still charging people £7 to get in. Someone I spoke to had just bribed the gate staff to let him in without a ticket - a reprehensible act, though appropriate punishment for corporate greed. After lunch, the Surrey opening pair knocked off the remainder of the runs. The last rites were conducted against the unusual bowling attack of Stevens and Sutcliffe. Kumble hardly turned an arm.

Surrey, Lancashire and Yorkshire all won their matches during the week, and were grouped together at the top of the table with only 14 points separating them. Leicestershire hung on to fourth place, but had lost to the leaders by an innings at Oakham, and 10 wickets at Guildford. They would need to lick their wounds and come out again strongly, or risk plunging into the relegation zone.

Leicestershire first innings

DL Maddy	c Batty	b Bicknell	3
IJ Sutcliffe	c Brown	b Bicknell	37
DI Stevens	c & b Bicknell		6
BF Smith	c Butcher	b Bicknell	102
A Habib	c Shahid	b Saqlain Mushtaq	20
*VJ Wells	lbw	b Bicknell	15
PAJ DeFreitas	c AJ Hollioake	b Saqlain Mushtaq	27
+ND Burns	c Batty	b Bicknell	4
D Williamson	c Batty	b AJ Hollioake	47
A Kumble	c Batty	b Bicknell	2
J Ormond	not out		2
Extras			53
Total	All Out		**318**

Bowling	O	M	R	W
Bicknell	28.1	5	72	7
Greenidge	12	2	35	0
BC Hollioake	19	5	74	0
Saqlain Mushtaq	39	9	93	2
AJ Hollioake	4	2	8	1
Salisbury	6	1	9	0

Surrey first innings

MA Butcher	c Burns	b Ormond	0
IJ Ward	c Habib	b DeFreitas	107
N Shahid	c Smith	b Kumble	47
*AJ Hollioake	c DeFreitas	b Ormond	18
AD Brown	c Burns	b Ormond	34
BC Hollioake	c Sutcliffe	b Ormond	21
+JN Batty	c Habib	b Kumble	3
MP Bicknell	lbw	b Ormond	0
IDK Salisbury	not out		10
Saqlain Mushtaq	c Habib	b Ormond	1
CG Greenidge	lbw	b Kumble	6
Extras			41
Total	All Out		**288**

Bowling	O	M	R	W
Ormond	29	6	87	6
DeFreitas	25	7	76	1
Wells	4	0	25	0
Williamson	6	0	17	0
Kumble	17	1	68	3

Leicestershire second innings

DL Maddy		b Bicknell	0
IJ Sutcliffe		b Bicknell	7
BF Smith	lbw	b Greenidge	8
DI Stevens	c Butcher	b Bicknell	14
+ND Burns	lbw	b Bicknell	0
A Habib	c Butcher	b Bicknell	2
*VJ Wells	c Brown	b Bicknell	17
PAJ DeFreitas	c Butcher	b Bicknell	24
D Williamson	not out		1
A Kumble	c BC Hollioake	b Bicknell	5
J Ormond		b Bicknell	0
Extras			9
Total	All Out		**87**

Bowling	O	M	R	W
Bicknell	12.5	3	47	9
Greenidge	11	6	35	1
Saqlain Mushtaq	1	0	2	0

Surrey second innings

MA Butcher	not out		47
IJ Ward	not out		61
Extras			11
Total	0 wickets		119

Bowling	O	M	R	W
Ormond	3	1	14	0
DeFreitas	15	2	30	0
Williamson	7	2	17	0
Kumble	3	1	5	0
Wells	4	1	13	0
Maddy	3	0	11	0
Stevens	3	0	8	0
Sutcliffe	1.3	0	12	0

Surrey won by 10 wickets. Points: Surrey 17, Leicestershire 6

11. Kent versus Leicestershire
Canterbury, 2 to 5 August

There can be few visitors who do not take a liking to the green Canterbury ground where Kent play most of their home cricket. The famous tree, inside the boundary rope, symbolises the rural character of the location. The element of informality (important to a cricket ground) is provided by lawns behind one bank of public seating, where a spectator can linger, glass in hand, to watch the play. The facilities and services are non-stuffy, and designed to be helpful. At the kiosk selling scorecards a blackboard carried the chalked message: "Leicestershire won the toss and chose to bat" - a useful feature which I had not seen elsewhere. Food is available from a variety of sources. The two scoreboards both have unique features: one is an unusual shape, and the other black on white.

Kent spectators were not to know it but, in compiling an opening stand of 39, Maddy and Sutcliffe gave Leicestershire an unusually positive start. Of 15 completed opening partnerships for the county during the season, 10 had registered fewer than 20 runs (four of these recording nought). Then Matthew Fleming, Kent's captain, brought himself on to bowl, and dismissed both openers leg before. "90 minutes of struggle," said a spectator, a trifle unkindly, when Sutcliffe went.

Matthew Walker, a lesser-known Kent player who was to make a contribution in this match, was given the over before lunch. He had bowled one ball when players and umpires made an indecently hasty rush for the pavilion, anticipating rain which never actually fell. The lunchtime score was 79 for 2. Ben Smith, resuming on 27, and with consecutive centuries under his belt, was clearly surprised to find himself caught behind off Walker. The Kent bowler has an unusual frame for a cricketer - short and heavy-limbed, so that from the boundary he resembles an overweight schoolboy. He was swinging the ball impressively for someone who, before the 2000 season, had no first-class wickets to his name.

Enter John Dakin, after a long lay-off for what one daily newspaper described as an "overhaul of general fitness", presumably a euphemism for, at the very least, 'losing weight'. Certainly his profile, as it ran from chest to knees, went in more of a straight line than its former 'question mark' shape. It was good to see Dakin in action again but, after striking a couple of powerful square fours, he swished unwisely at a wide ball from Saggers and was caught behind for 10.

The score was 98 for 4 when Vince Wells came to the wicket, at the club which had 'let him go' nine years earlier. As with most players in this situation Wells no doubt felt he had something to prove, and from the start of this innings he looked in his best form of the season. He is never a classically elegant player but, like Kent's captain, Matthew Fleming, to whom he bears some resemblance in both appearance and playing record, he can biff the ball hard, often by the aerial route. One of these lofted drives just cleared extra cover, striking the fielder's finger-tips and running on for two, and Wells was twice dropped off other half chances. When his score reached 27 he overtook Aftab Habib, who had preceded him at the crease. He chalked up 50 with a square drive which swirled off the bat, just eluding a fielder, and crossing the boundary after one bounce; the shot typified his style of play.

Habib was in unusually defensive mode in his Canterbury innings, resisting scoring shots other than singles; but his strokes - whether aggressive or defensive - are invariably elegant and precise. Like many people who are really good at something, Habib is transformed when batting. Seen around the ground at Grace Road - where he often sits in the public seating - he can seem heavy in body, and rather glum. At the crease he is all lightness, like a dancer, and full of certainty. Batting is what he does.

Tea was taken at 194 for 4, with Wells on 55 and Habib 47. As things turned out, the stand between them was the biggest of the match. An early threat of rain had given way to a pleasant, sunny evening, though periodic gusts of wind transformed the trees around the ground into a moving frieze, and sent hats twirling. One of these, falling on the outfield, was retrieved during play by a man in cavernous, astonishingly loose trousers, which defied gravity in not falling around his ankles, while he clutched in desperation at their perimeter. The crowd gave him a round of applause.

Notwithstanding this incident, it was a sedate day's play, both on and off the pitch, featuring little gee-up shouting from the Kent players, and the least jingoistic crowd I had encountered so far. Next to me, a girl of about seven remarked to a boy of the same age: "I do get fed up with cricket - it's a bit boring". And there was an extraordinary conversation between two Kent members about the colour of cricket clothing, apparently the lifelong study of one of them. "Whites came in around 1880," he observed; before that, "Lord

Harris like to play in blue". "The only team that stayed in coloured shirts were Rugby School, I think," he said, with the nonchalance of the anorak.

By tea the character of the match was defined. Nixon - the former Leicestershire wicketkeeper - was standing up to most of the Kent bowlers, including Walker, Mark Ealham, a young, medium-fast bowler David Masters and, of course, the spinner Min Patel. The pitch was slowish, and without noticeable lateral movement. Ealham bowled to just one slip at 5.30pm. It was surprising that the first close fielder in front of the wicket appeared just before close of play, to Patel. Wells fell lbw to Ealham for 72, and DeFreitas struck a brisk 16, but Habib retired into his shell for much of the last session, particularly in the closing overs. At the close, 263 for 6, he was on 78; one felt that he might regret not pushing on to his century, with his eye in against tired bowling.

In the evening, at a pleasant inn, the Anchor House, just outside the city walls, I found that all but one of the guests were there for the cricket. One large party included a man who had travelled in for the Canterbury week game for the past 14 years. Another retired couple were from the Sussex coast; they often watched games at Hove ("a concrete slab"), but not having a car, were unable to reach several of the locations that Sussex used. During the summer, I found that transport was a recurring preoccupation for less prosperous cricket fans.

Second day

On the second day, heavy overnight rain delayed the start of play until after lunch, and an ominous forecast shed doubt upon prospects for the afternoon. I went down to the ground at lunchtime and paid my £8. As at Grace Road, the side entrance to the ground is along a tiny dirt track on a suburban street, completely unsigned. Blink and you miss it. "That's our little secret, that is," said the attendant at the 'gate', with his small table, box for cash, and striped umbrella to keep off the rain - the high-tech environment of county cricket.

Spectators got three overs before play was interrupted. A colossal black cloud had drifted over the ground - "that evil bugger" - said a spectator and, at the first drop of water spectators in the open public seating scattered like wasps disturbed from a jam jar. Immediately, the sky dumped its contents onto the pitch, to a prolonged accompaniment of thunder and lightning. There would clearly be no further play for several hours at least. Despite the gloom, and the drop in temperature, I could imagine few more agreeable places than Canterbury cricket ground to be - to sit and read, sip a cup of tea, or talk to other spectators. According to temperament, people feel most at peace in different locations: in a church, in a garden, on a mountain or a river bank, and so on. For some it is hard to beat a cricket ground; come to that, the outfield of Canterbury or Grace Road would suit my ashes nicely.

An alternative entertainment of sorts was provided. I had not initially registered that a ladies' day 'hat competition' was under way, and the first batches of contestants to emerge from the hospitality tents and pick their way through mud churned up by the wheels of Rovers and Daimlers were a startling sight - like kingfishers glimpsed flitting across a swamp. Had the ladies perhaps got on the wrong train for Goodwood? One woman had a clock on her head. Another advised her companion: "It's all a question of timing with the feather". You half expected the Queen Mother to appear.

Play restarted at 5.30pm, with two to three hundred die-hards in the ground. The surprise feature of the hour's session, just long enough to deny spectators any refund on their tickets, was the batting of Anil Kumble. There had been rumours that he could bat, bolstered by his first class batting average of 27, which encompassed six centuries. Leicestershire followers were strangers to all of this, for the Indian's scores for the county before the Kent match were 1, 15, 0, 4, 2, 0, 10, 0, 2, 0, 3 and 1. For once, instead of blasting away on arrival, he began cautiously, as though rediscovering some skill buried deep in his consciousness, like riding a bicycle. He was urged by his partner Burns to run harder, turning ones into twos, and twos into threes, and slowly warmed to his task, to the point where he almost seemed to be enjoying himself. Just before Burns was caught and bowled by Patel, the pair marked up a 50 partnership. When play ended with Leicestershire 324 for 8, Kumble was still there on 32.

Third day

The third day was again delayed by a heavy shower and play began under cloud cover. Kumble continued to play a range of shots around the wicket, and reached his half century with a fine leg-side deflection to the boundary. The landmark was cheered by his colleagues in the pavilion without a hint of irony. As if to celebrate, Kumble demonstrated an extraordinary shot, bringing the bat downwards from a vertical position above his head, like a tennis smash - though all this effort and invention yielded only a single to mid-wicket. When he was finally caught at long off by Ealham, Kumble had made 67 - virtually double his previous number of runs for the season.

The Leicestershire total was 375. All of the 'out' batsmen had reached double figures, and their last three wickets added 133. Late order scoring for the Midlands county happens so frequently that it is almost taken for granted. Wells must sometimes be tempted to reverse his batting order. Saggers was the pick of the Kent bowling and, perhaps significantly - in an attack which lacked pace - the fastest. Patel's spin was disappointing, especially when compared to the spin to come.

I had got talking to a man in his 70s, who had travelled up from Catford. Cricket followers, coming in all shapes, sizes and classes, resist diagnosis until conversation reveals their quiet fanaticism. I asked the man what drew him to the game, but like many enthusiasts he could not pin it down. His father had been "obsessive", and the son "got the bug"; he had played a lot, and now umpired. Transport problems and, though he did not exactly say so, increasing infirmity, were the main obstacles to watching these days. The man failed a sort of 'reverse Tebbitt test'. He was identifying England possibles from the Leicestershire team (Maddy, Ben Smith) when I reminded him of Habib. "Oh well... I mean... the *real* English players... you know..." Needless to say, I did not agree with him.

With just about five sessions left for play in this match the odds were on a draw, though the Leicestershire tail's rapid scoring had given their team an outside chance of bowling Kent out cheaply and enforcing the follow-on. A Kent win seemed to be out of the question.

It became clear early in Kent's first innings that Kumble would extract more from the slow pitch than any other bowler on either side. Wells brought him on after only six overs of Ormond and DeFreitas, and he soon dismissed both openers: Fulton was lbw going only half forward, and Key watched the Indian's top spin take the ball gently onto the stumps from a forward defensive stroke.

Many spectators in the decent crowd would have been there to watch Rahul Dravid bat and he began in style, striking Ormond through the on-side field and, two balls later, through the covers. In quick time came a boundary from a square cut off the same bowler, then a drive to square leg from Kumble, almost from a forward defensive posture. The elegance and certainty of these strokes put him immediately into a different class from other batsmen seen in the match. He was also a very good, quick judge of a run. Dravid's exercises between overs, which at one point resembled the hokey-kokey, contrasted strangely with the elegance of his stoke-play.

After this early flurry of strokes the Indian batsman put the brakes on and contented himself with singles, yielding the strike to his partner. Ed Smith kept pace with his illustrious companion, and in mid-afternoon the 50 partnership was passed. At this point Kumble had been bowling for two hours uninterrupted, but he now gave way to the new, slim-line Dakin, who bounded in from long leg to take the ball. That Dakin bowls 'a heavy ball' was soon attested to by that peculiar dull thud of ball on bat which often occurs when he is operating. Nevertheless it was a surprise when he had Dravid lbw on his crease - the batsman's punishment, perhaps, for losing the initiative after an innings which began so impressively.

After tea, taken at 97 for 3, Dakin also had Smith caught at the wicket. With Mark Ealham coming to the wicket at 108 for 4, Leicestershire may have seen themselves closing in for the kill. The Canterbury crowd's lack of confidence in their team's batting - rivalled only by the diffidence of the Durham crowd - would have been a further encouragement. There then occurred an incident which, in retrospect, may have had a big influence on the outcome of the match. Carl Crowe, in the middle of a long and excellent spell of off-spin bowling, found Matthew Walker adrift in the middle of the pitch after a mix-up with Ealham. Any kind of respectable throw to Burns would have ended Walker's innings, but Crowe lost his head and hurled the ball wildly at the wicket, missing by such a margin that the batsmen ran three overthrows.

Leicestershire made progress at the other end when Sutcliffe took the first of several catches at silly mid-on to dismiss Ealham off Crowe. We had the unusual sight - for Leicestershire - of spinners at both ends, imposing a stranglehold in the Surrey mould. Kumble bowled with four men round the bat, and it was Sutcliffe at silly mid-off who comfortably accounted for Nixon. After Matthew Fleming had struck some violent blows he too was caught by Sutcliffe, off the bowling of Ormond.

On a sunny evening Leicestershire struggled to set up a conclusive position for an assault on the Kent batting during the last day. They needed to impose the follow-on, of course, but I also felt that they had to dismiss Kent before close of play - because taking 10 wickets on an unresponsive fourth-day pitch was challenge enough. In the event they could not quite manage it. Kent finished on 184 for 8, still 42 behind the total needed to avoid the follow-on. Matthew Walker, who might have been run out an hour earlier, remained on 36.

Fourth day

On the fourth day - which I did not see - Kent held out for a draw. They were dismissed for 201, followed on, and reached 187 for 7 in their second innings. Robert Key scored a half century, before playing on in exactly the same manner as in the first innings, and Matthew Walker was again not out, for 24. Anil Kumble took six wickets from 33 overs, and Carl Crowe the other wicket to fall, off 25 overs.

Leicestershire ended this round of first division matches fifth in the table, just seven points ahead of Kent in sixth position - with neither team very far from the three relegation positions. Kent supporters could frequently be heard discussing the prospect of "the drop". Both Kent and Leicestershire had won three matches out of 10, but the latter could claim, with every justification, that they had again been deprived of a victory by the weather. They outplayed Kent, and looked a stronger side in both bowling and batting. The return of Dakin contributed greatly to the balance of the team. Carl Crowe bowled 38 overs in the match and, with the returning Dakin, gave Leicestershire their best hand of bowling options so far in the season.

On the debit side Leicestershire had again failed to win a match away from Grace Road. Even their match at Oakham School had ended in defeat. They appeared to have a confidence on their home pitch which eluded them elsewhere. Their next chance to rectify this was to be at Southampton the following week.

Leicestershire first innings

					Bowling	O	M	R	W
DL Maddy	lbw		b Fleming	22	Saggers	33.5	10	70	4
IJ Sutcliffe	lbw		b Fleming	15	Masters	32	7	92	1
BF Smith	c Nixon		b Walker	27	Ealham	22	6	56	1
A Habib	c Nixon		b Saggers	78	Fleming	13	1	54	2
JM Dakin	c Nixon		b Saggers	10	Walker	10	3	18	1
*VJ Wells	lbw		b Ealham	72	Patel	20	6	65	1
PAJ DeFreitas	lbw		b Masters	16	Dravid	3	2	1	0
A Kumble	c Ealham	b Saggers		56					
+ND Burns	c & b Patel			23					
CD Crowe	c Nixon		b Saggers	12					
J Ormond	not out			9					
Extras				35					
Total	All Out			**375**					

Kent first innings

					Bowling	O	M	R	W
DP Fulton	lbw	b Kumble	11		Bowling	O	M	R	W
RWT Key		b Kumble	14		Ormond	22.2	10	57	3
R Dravid	lbw	b Dakin	32		DeFreitas	10	5	13	0
ET Smith	c Burns	b Dakin	40		Kumble	32	9	61	4
MJ Walker	not out		48		Wells	4	0	15	0
MA Ealham	c Sutcliffe	b Crowe	6		Dakin	7	1	20	2
+PA Nixon	c Sutcliffe	b Kumble	2		Crowe	13	5	26	1
*MV Fleming	c Sutcliffe	b Ormond	18						
MM Patel	c Maddy	b Ormond	8						
DD Masters	c Smith	b Kumble	0						
MJ Saggers	lbw	b Ormond	1						
Extras			21						
Total	All Out		**201**						

Kent second innings

					Bowling	O	M	R	W
DP Fulton	c Smith	b Kumble	21		Bowling	O	M	R	W
RWT Key		b Kumble	53		Ormond	10	3	28	0
R Dravid	c Smith	b Kumble	24		DeFreitas	10	3	34	0
ET Smith	c Smith	b Kumble	13		Dakin	7	4	7	0
MJ Walker	not out		24		Kumble	33	13	44	6
MA Ealham		b Kumble	3		Crowe	25	6	56	1
+PA Nixon		b Crowe	1						
*MV Fleming	lbw	b Kumble	5						
MM Patel	not out		5						
Extras			38						
Total	7 wickets		**187**						

Match drawn. Points: Leicestershire 11, Kent 8

104

12. Hampshire versus Leicestershire
Southampton, 8 to 11 August

Any visit to the home of Hampshire cricket this year had to have an elegiac quality, because the Northlands Road site is being supplanted by the new 'West End' ground in 2001. Change is painful, but not necessarily for everyone. "Is it a good move?" I asked my cab driver. "It's good for me. The fare to the present ground is about £4. At the new one it'll be about £8." "Not good for the punters, then?", I said. "I try not to think about that," he replied.

Northlands Road suits Southampton in the way that the Canterbury ground suits its home city. It is intimate and suburban. The stands and pavilion, constructed in 1895, are low, as are the surrounding houses. Even the trees are low. The imminent move has encouraged a run-down appearance, which the ubiquitous beige seating does not improve. The somewhat ramshackle stands look better from the far side of the ground than from within. One feature needing improvement next year is the congested and confusing main scoreboard.

At some stage, it was not clear when, the planned date of this fixture was brought forward by one day. The unfortunate visiting supporter has little hope of discovering such alterations in advance. I spotted the fixture announcement in the morning paper at 9am and dashed off to Southampton, arriving just after the lunch interval. Leicestershire were 95 for 2, with Maddy and Smith out, Sutcliffe just about to reach his half-century, and Habib already well set.

'Mistaken identity' was a feature of the afternoon session. Soon after my arrival, as I tried to disentangle information from the scoreboard, a Hampshire member advised: "You don't want to take too much notice of what it says up there." As he spoke, the announcer made a second revision to the identity of the substitute fielder. "Dear, oh dear, oh dear," lamented the member's wife. "You'd think he'd know our own players." Getting this right was to prove important, for on 53 Sutcliffe hooked violently at Morris, and the substitute fielder hared along the boundary from long leg and flung himself forward to take the ball two-handed before it crossed the boundary boards for six. Amid warm applause the announcer ventured a further correction: the fielder's name was Shah. It was the player's one stab at fame because, of course all the published reports would carry the anodyne legend "c sub b Morris".

The minor confusion was followed by another as Sutcliffe's replacement - Darren Stevens - was identified on the scoreboard as Vince Wells. A Leicestershire member, out of his natural element and horrified at the ways of southerners, was incandescent, and upbraided the scoreboard operator during an hour-long break for rain. "Are you sure about this?" said the operator. "I've been a Leicestershire member for 28 years - I should know our own players," the man raged. It was an easy mistake to make because the two batsmen look very similar at the crease - as many players do of similar height, togged up in the same gear with the same county cap, and so on. The vital clue was only apparent when Wells did come out to join Stevens at the crease, and reveal his legs-apart stance, in contrast to the more reticent, legs-together stance of Stevens. The seeds of doubt had been sown; when Stevens was out to the first of many diving catches by Aymes, members filling in their scorecards were still muttering: "Now was that Stevens... or Wells?"

Habib had been going tremendously well before the rain break, reaching 61 in no time at all. He was caught behind first ball after the resumption, just as he had after a rain break at Canterbury. Many of his dismissals result from catches by the wicket-keeper and slip cordon.

Hampshire had Shane Warne absent on duty for Australia, but another top-class bowler was fit and able. Alan Mullally (lately of Leicestershire) was in the middle of a tremendous bout of form, having taken 14 wickets in his previous match. The Leicestershire coach, Jack Birkenshaw, was quoted in the press next morning speaking about the green-top wicket Hampshire had prepared for Mullally's bowling. In fact the pitch seemed to swing more than seam, and Mullally outswingers had accounted for both Maddy and Ben Smith in the morning session. In the middle of a long bowl he also had Wells out lbw for 22.

Dakin's appearance drew the sort of comment from home supporters, "Just look at the size of him", that would normally have been reserved for the Egyptian pyramids, or the Empire State Building. A woman looked him up in the *Playfair Cricket Annual*. "Six foot four. And he's quite young - 27 in February." "He's still growing," said her husband. The reverse was true; what would they have said about him before the "general fitness overhaul"?

At 169 for 6, Leicestershire's usual habit - a poor start followed by consolidation - was being inverted. Dakin's bulk provided reassurance. Such is his height and reach that he tends to go only half forward in defence, but that is generally enough. He punched a short ball from Mullally square for four. The next delivery was overpitched and Dakin pushed at it mildly, watching the ball outstrip the fielders to the long-on boundary. Next over he hit Mascarenhas through the covers on the up. The sound of Dakin's bat is different from that of the touch players in the Leicestershire team: a heavy bat to go with the 'heavy ball' that he bowls.

Like Wells before him, Dominic Williamson was out lbw to a Mullally inswinger. Burns replaced him, but left-handedness was no protection. Bowling to five slips - an unusual sight in county cricket - Mullally needed none of them, having him caught by a diving Aymes behind the wicket.

Leicestershire were 189 for 8. It was a losing score, yet the county's supporters have become almost blasé about early and middle-innings collapses, certain that at some stage of the proceedings two players will come together and bale the team out. The 24-year old off-spinner, Carl Crowe, joined Dakin at the wicket on what was by now a fine summer evening. Together they negotiated the final overs of Mullally's prolonged spell, alleviating defence with an occasional scoring shot. From nowhere, Crowe played a lordly on drive for four, drawing a "glorious shot" from my neighbour. As at Canterbury the week before, these spectators were noticeably ungrudging in applause for their opponents. Dakin hooked Morris very hard to the square-leg boundary, then turned a single square for his 50.

Shaun Udal, Hampshire's spinner, took the ball for the first time in the day at 6.30pm, but Dakin hit a long hop through the covers, and Crowe flicked another boundary to long-leg. Just before the close Dakin was picked up at slip off John Stephenson. He had made 60, and the stand of 71 with Crowe had taken Leicestershire to semi-respectability at 265 for 9. Leicestershire fans had known it would happen all along.

Arriving in Southampton at short notice can be problematic, because beds are almost as hard to find as at Guildford. I phoned round guest-houses from the ground and got a basic, but expensive, room in an inn near the docks.

Second day

On the second morning, under heavy cloud cover, Hampshire soon polished off the last Leicestershire wicket. Carl Crowe made a very creditable 26 in a total of 266. Mullally had bowled 28 overs, and taken 5 for 84.

Predictions about the Hampshire innings were even more difficult than these things usually are. The county's position at the bottom of the First Division table was down to their batting. They had registered a sad average of one batting bonus point per game during the season. Against this was the remarkably unfortunate situation that all of Leicestershire's front-line bowlers were absent: Ormond, DeFreitas, and Kumble were all injured (and Chris Lewis rarely turned out anyway). The bowling would rest upon Dakin, Boswell, Wells, Crowe and Williamson. It was hard to imagine this relatively untried quintet bowling out even Hampshire twice in the match.

Dakin opened the bowling with both lift and pace, prompting regret at the absence of speedometers on county grounds. Kendall chopped on to a lifter, and Derek Kenway was given out leg before. Kendall, cutting, was badly dropped by Stevens at deep point, but then played down the wrong line to Boswell and was bowled. Boswell also had Jason Laney splendidly caught by a diving Wells at slip. Hampshire were 64 for 4. Robin Smith soon demonstrated that his favourite square cut was in working order, and also coaxed a ball from Wells delightfully through the covers. When Dominic Williamson bowled, Smith crashed him square on one knee, but then reached forward to an outswinger to give Wells another catch. It was sad to see this continued confirmation of Smith's poor season. A Hampshire supporter said that he thought Smith's eyesight was beginning to go - the sort of speculation that cannot be verified.

After lunch Aymes and Mascarenhas put together the first respectable partnership, in their very different styles. Aymes is a gritty batsman who gives nothing away, and plays within his limitations. In complete contrast, Mascarenhas strikes the ball flamboyantly, and knows no other way. He dealt severely with Williamson, twice thumping him through the covers, and once straight off the back foot. Dakin was pulled and cut for boundaries. Wells brought himself back into the attack. He had bowled a testing spell in the morning without luck, inducing much playing and missing, and now bowled Mascarenhas as he attempted another fierce drive. The partnership had put on just over 50, in a total of 124 for 6.

Carl Crowe ushered spin into the attack at 3pm. In the middle of a long, economical spell Stephenson skied him to mid-off where Wells, in an unusual fielding position for him, took a third catch. When Udal was caught behind off Boswell, Hampshire were in familiar territory - 173 for 8.

Alex Morris, back in the Hampshire team after a long absence through injury, came in at number 10 and immediately looked too good for that lowly position - especially when he pulled Crowe to the mid-wicket boundary. A much-needed partnership developed as Aymes proceeded with great confidence, notably strong through the covers and through deflections to long leg. The innings was almost an exact repeat of his effort at Grace Road earlier in the season, where he had come in at 61 for 4, and scored 74 in a team total of 229. At Southampton he came to the crease at 64 for 4, and scored 71 in a total of 228. He was finally out after tea, well caught by Burns off an inside edge from Wells. Seeing Mullally come to the wicket Morris immediately struck out powerfully to the square leg boundary, but found Smith plucking the ball out of the air to end the innings. The story relayed by Hampshire spectators - no doubt for the umpteenth time - was that a friend of Mullally's had once phoned him at the ground, to be told that he had just gone out to bat. "I'll hold on then, shall I?" the friend is supposed to have said.

Leicestershire's first inning lead was 38. Their second string bowlers had done their coach proud, imaginatively handled by Wells, and bowling to aggressive field settings. Boswell took the eye with 3 for 39 in 15 overs. Crowe, bowling with excellent control, sent down 14 overs for 28 runs. Wells put in his best bowling of the season, and took 3 for 39 in 20 overs. Hampshire had batted poorly, Aymes, Mascarenhas and Morris excepted. The dark side for Leicestershire was that they could not expect Hampshire to bat as poorly again, or their untried bowlers to do as well.

In an hour's batting for Leicestershire that evening, Maddy and Sutcliffe made a good start, putting on 42 without loss or any apparent difficulty.

Third day

Maddy fell lbw to his first ball from Mascarenhas the following morning, playing down the wrong line. Hampshire opened with their two most penetrative bowlers: Mascarenhas and Mullally, bowling from the opposite end to the one in the first innings where he had taken five wickets. This was unusual. Also strange was that he began his spell with a single slip - a peculiarity soon punished as Ben Smith snicked a ball at perfect catching height precisely through the second slip area. The lapse was not to prove costly, for Mullally soon removed Smith's off stump, making the batsman kick angrily at his crease before departing. Sutcliffe, who had been driving Mascarenhas to distraction by playing and missing outside the off stump, swished and was well caught by Aymes diving to his left. It was 72 for 3.

Hampshire appear to have a wonderful prospect in Dimitri Mascarenhas. Here was an example of statistics giving little idea of a player's potential. In 39 previous first class matches the all-rounder had scored nearly 1,200 runs at an average of 23.7, and taken 71 wickets at just over 36 per wicket. But the player was only 22, and his career was in front of him. He had batted with a dash that enlivened the Hampshire innings, and was clearly regarded in this match as his team's second bowler after Mullally. Twenty overs in Leicestershire's first innings were followed by 23 in the second, all probing and aggressive. His further exploits will be watched with great interest, not least by the selectors of the England team, for which he is qualified to play.

Despite the entrance of Stevens, the scoring rate fell to just more than two an over. A Hampshire supporter remarked that he had never seen so many leave-alones in the first period of play. Much of this was due to uncertainty induced by Mullally, who bowled 16 overs unchanged throughout the morning, swinging the ball both ways, and still kicking up his heels just before delivery in his boyish, unmistakable manner. He had Habib caught at slip, and Stevens caught by the wicket-keeper, diving once more. After lunch Mullally came back again, until Morris eventually replaced him at 2.25pm.

Even then Mullally contrived to stay in the game. He is not renowned for his fielding - rather the reverse - but when Dakin pushed to deep mid-off and ran, Mullally threw down the wicket at the bowler's end with an accurate strike. Of course, as former team mates they knew each other well. Perhaps Dakin was thinking: "It's only Alan - I can risk it"; if so, Mullally may have seen Dakin lumbering down the pitch and thought: "Even I can run him out". It was 129 for 6.

As each wicket fell, away supporters would have been adding 38 - Leicestershire's first inning lead - to their team's total to calculate the score Hampshire needed in their second innings, and thinking: "It's not enough!" Mullally, back at 2.55pm after only half an hour's rest, struck again by having Wells caught behind off another outstanding Aymes catch. Meanwhile Burns was playing a most uncharacteristic innings, mixing fierce square cuts with hoicks to long on, and scoring at a rate that would have delighted a Stevens or a Mascarenhas. He was the one-man answer to a Hampshire supporter's fully justified comment: "There's been no adventure

110

in the Leicestershire batting, has there?" It all ended in tears when Burns dashed down the wicket while facing Udal and was stumped.

That was the icing on the cake in a wonderful match for wicket-keeper Adrian Aymes. As well as the stumping, and making the highest score of the match, he took eight catches - many of them from a horizontal position a few inches from the ground. Most impressive of all, perhaps, he permitted a single bye during two innings in which the Hampshire bowlers had sprayed the ball all around the crease, frequently drawing applause for spectacular stops. All this, by the way, from a man of 36. Yet spectacular is not what Aymes is about; he is the original gritty and undemonstrative team player.

After Carl Crowe was bowled by Stephenson, Leicestershire were 175 for 9, and had an overall lead of 213. Plainly, this was not enough. Most observers felt that the pitch had eased, and the Leicestershire second-string bowlers could hardly be expected to perform as well as in the first innings. A lead of 220 seemed an absolute minimum, while 250 would give a reasonable chance of victory. The desirable target - 300 - was light years away.

When Boswell joined Williamson for the last wicket, the 'significant stand' which the Leicestershire lower order normally produced had not happened. The Leicestershire scorecard looked like a support case for the fiercest critics of English batting technique. All the batsmen except Dakin made a start by reaching double figures, but none went beyond Sutcliffe's 37; in fact, Sutcliffe apart, they were all out for between 13 and 23.

Mullally returned to the attack to finish off the innings. The details of his spells during the day are worth recording again: he bowled for the whole of the morning session (from 11am to 1.15pm; after lunch from 1.55 to 2.25; again from 2.55 to 3.50; and finally from 4.10 to 4.30. These marathon contributions added up to 37 overs, during which he took 4 for 59. Not bad for a man frequently described as "laid back".

For once Mullally did not take a wicket on his return, and Williamson and Boswell began to put together a stand: nothing dramatic - some pushed singles, and the occasional cautious drive into the covers for two or three. Williamson has an excellent bash-to-long-on stroke which he had deployed at Guildford, and now unwrapped again. The crowd became slightly restive as they awaited the end, but continued to applaud Leicestershire strokes with undiminished good manners. Boswell tried their patience severely by thrice snicking through the slip cordon for four. When Williamson charged Udal and was dropped at slip (Udal's safe hands no longer being there), someone's patience snapped, and an anguished cry of "for Christ's sake" betrayed the tension in the stands. In the next over Boswell repeated this trick, and this time Kendall hung on at slip to dismiss him for 20. Williamson had his team's highest score of 43, out of a total of 240. Hampshire's target to win was 279.

Hampshire had 23 overs of batting left on the day, and I moved into the small stand of covered public seating to watch it. This was a cramped, unprepossessing structure, underpinned by green metal girders placed too close together, as though constructed by a 10-year-old from an old Meccano set. The roof girders were decorated with liberal helpings of bird droppings. The denizens of the stand had a weathered appearance that suggested long months of incumbency. As at most cricket venues, they reflected all elements of the social structure. Anoraks and baggy cardigans were rife, but there was also a man in a boater smoking a cigar. Another man wearing an MCC tie allowed his bottom set of false teeth to drop down like the visor in a suit of armour - a solecism which, if repeated at Lords, might have meant a life-long ban from the club. At the front of the stand, a well-dressed man had removed brogues and socks, and dabbled his bare feet on the grass verge. A large young bloke behind me was inviting his companion to a "root crop party". "You go dressed as a root crop," he said lugubriously, by way of explanation. "Larry's going as a cabbage."

The last innings of the match began with Dakin and Boswell bowling at the Hampshire openers. When the score reached 14 Kenway lashed out at a short ball from Dakin, sending a towering hit way beyond mid-off. Carl Crowe, fielding in this position, turned and hared off in the direction of the hit, arrived as the ball fell to earth, and took the catch calmly over his shoulder; he never looked like dropping it. The excellence of the fielding did not distract attention from the inappropriate stroke, execrated by the Hampshire chairman, who was sitting out in the stands: "Bloody silly shot," was his reaction. Before the close, for bad light, Kendall was out lbw to a ball from Wells which squirted. Morris came in as night-watchman, and helped White to take the score to 54 for 2.

Fourth day

The last day (or half day) of the match exemplified the uncertainties of cricket. Early on, White and Morris took Hampshire's score to 144 for 2, in a stand of 99. White reached a deserved half century, but it was night-watchman Morris who took everyone's eye, as he pulled, cut and on-drove the Leicestershire attack attractively for 12 boundaries, in an innings lasting two and three-quarter hours. Morris, normally the Hampshire number 10, had also featured in his team's biggest stand in the first innings (54 with Aymes). He looked the part in both innings, and one wondered why Hampshire did not play him at second wicket down for a whole match.

The day's cricket turned on two overs before lunch. Williamson can seem a harmless bowler, and an expensive one, but he has a surprise ball which moves away from the right-handed batsman; White was bowled by it for 50. In the next over Carl Crowe found the edge of Morris's bat with an off-spinner, and Ben Smith took an easy slip catch. With Hampshire 144 for 4, facing a target of 279, the odds were slightly in favour of the away team.

After lunch the worst fears of the home crowd were realised. Carl Crowe was the main agent of destruction. His career could be presented as a symptom of England's spinning problems. He made his debut for Leicestershire in 1995, but had bowled a mere 550 overs before the beginning of the season, taking 17 wickets. As soon as the county's premier spinner, Brimson, retired, Kumble turned up as the overseas player, and has been almost an ever-present in the Leicestershire team. Not surprisingly, Crowe's opportunities have been limited. Spinners need to bowl. At Canterbury, where Leicestershire fielded Kumble and Crowe on a mildly turning pitch, the 24-year-old bowled a total of 38 overs. Though he took only two wickets there, the long stint had quite clearly increased his confidence. The spell of 21 consecutive overs in the second innings at Southampton was marked by close control, and yielded his best ever return of 4 for 55. He had a bit of luck, as Aymes pulled a short ball to mid-wicket. Then Robin Smith cut and edged, and Burns somehow trapped the ball (bouncing off his chin) near his thigh. Finally Crowe caught and bowled Laney off a leading edge.

Vince Wells ended the Hampshire innings with another captain's bowling performance. Hampshire, finishing on 217, were 61 runs short. Had they emulated Leicestershire's last wicket partnership they would still have won the match, but that is not how things have gone for them this year. One of their members was apoplectic at the close, crying out bitterly at the home team's balcony.

Notwithstanding Hampshire's problems, enormous credit was due to the away team, in what had to be their best performance of the year. Leicestershire had been forced to field a second-string attack, further depleted in the second innings when Dakin pulled a muscle early on the fourth morning. Nothing daunted, they twice bowled the opposition out. The Leicestershire management and coach must have been absolutely delighted with the three younger players, who had all made important contributions. Boswell took three wickets in the first innings, and was a component of the match-winning last-wicket stand. Williamson was the leading batsman in that stand, and also took an important wicket in each innings. Crowe bowled exceptionally well, scored 25 in the first innings, and pouched a steepling, difficult catch.

The image of the game for me was Scott Boswell running from long-leg to deep square-leg to turn a Hampshire boundary into only two runs. The big man forced his large frame to go flat out, grunting furiously and his face was contorted with the effort of reaching the ball in time. He hurled his body to the ground so that the ball had no chance of eluding him, and threw back above the stumps. Effort - professionalism - character - Leicestershire.

Leicestershire first innings

DL Maddy	c Kendall	b Mullally	8
IJ Sutcliffe	c sub	b Morris	53
BF Smith	c Aymes	b Mullally	5
A Habib	c Aymes	b Mascarenhas	61
DI Stevens	c Aymes	b Mascarenhas	12
*VJ Wells	lbw	b Mullally	22
JM Dakin	c Laney	b Stephenson	60
D Williamson	lbw	b Mullally	4
+ND Burns	c Aymes	b Mullally	0
CD Crowe	c Aymes	b Morris	26
SAJ Boswell	not out		5
Extras			10
Total	All Out		**266**

Bowling	O	M	R	W
Mullally	28	6	84	5
Morris	18.3	2	54	2
Stephenson	13	1	49	1
Mascarenhas	20	4	59	2
Udal	4	0	16	0

Hampshire first innings

GW White		b Dakin	2
DA Kenway	lbw	b Dakin	8
WS Kendall		b Boswell	20
*RA Smith	c Wells	b Williamson	15
JS Laney	c Wells	b Boswell	15
+AN Aymes	c Burns	b Wells	71
AD Mascarenhas		b Wells	34
JP Stephenson	c Wells	b Crowe	14
SD Udal	c Burns	b Boswell	12
AC Morris	c Smith	b Wells	19
AD Mullally	not out		1
Extras			17
Total	All Out		**228**

Bowling	O	M	R	W
Dakin	21	3	70	2
Boswell	15	4	39	3
Wells	20	6	39	3
Williamson	7	0	37	1
Crowe	14	3	28	1
Maddy	4	0	12	0

Leicestershire second innings

DL Maddy	lbw	b Mascarenhas	18
IJ Sutcliffe	c Aymes	b Mascarenhas	37
BF Smith		b Mullally	15
A Habib	c Udal	b Mullally	13
DI Stevens	c Aymes	b Mullally	24
*VJ Wells	c Aymes	b Mullally	20
JM Dakin	run out		8
+ND Burns	st Aymes	b Udal	23
D Williamson	not out		43
CD Crowe		b Stephenson	2
SAJ Boswell	c Kendall	b Udal	20
Extras			17
Total	All Out		**240**

Bowling	O	M	R	W
Mullally	37	15	59	4
Morris	11	3	22	0
Stephenson	10	0	51	1
Udal	15.3	5	36	2
Mascarenhas	23	5	65	2

Hampshire second innings

GW White		b Williamson	50
DA Kenway	c Crowe	b Dakin	7
WS Kendall	lbw	b Wells	16
AC Morris	c Smith	b Crowe	60
*RA Smith	c Burns	b Crowe	20
JS Laney	c & b Crowe		6
+AN Aymes	c Maddy	b Crowe	6
AD Mascarenhas	not out		27
JP Stephenson	c Burns	b Wells	5
SD Udal	lbw	b Wells	1
AD Mullally	c Sutcliffe	b Wells	0
Extras			19
Total	All Out		**217**

Bowling	O	M	R	W
Dakin	7	1	29	1
Boswell	12	3	30	0
Wells	20.4	4	54	4
Crowe	27	7	55	4
Williamson	13	2	42	1

Leicestershire won by 61 runs. Points: Leicestershire 17, Hampshire 4

The team room at Grace Road. The picture windows offer the best view
in the ground (Photo: Sylvia Michael)

13. Leicestershire versus Yorkshire
Grace Road, 16 to 19 August

A decent crowd turned out on a fresh, sunny first morning at Grace Road, following two consecutive away matches for the county team. Prospects of play against the Yorkshire side currently running second in the championship prompted a distinct buzz of anticipation among spectators. But was this really Yorkshire? A glance at the scorecard revealed a list of unfamiliar names that could have belonged to a village team misdirected to the Grace Road venue. In part this was down to the Test match starting the next day. The old saying "a strong Yorkshire means a strong England" could be rephrased to run "a strong England means a weak Yorkshire". Vaughan, White, Gough and Hoggard were all in the national squad. Injured absentees included two more seamers, Hutchison and Sidebottom, and the captain Byas. The wicket-keeper Blakey had apparently been dropped.

With all these fast bowlers absent, Yorkshire still fielded two who had played for England: Silverwood and Hamilton. Despite this pedigree, they both bowled badly in the first hour, spraying the ball all over the wicket. The first wide, from Hamilton, in the 12th over, could have been called earlier. Ten of the first 25 runs scored were extras, and there would have been more had not the young wicket-keeper, Simon Guy, dived around his crease like the goalkeeper of an amateur team facing Manchester United in a cup tie.

The second string bowlers took over rather sooner than Yorkshire might have planned. Elstub and Gary Fellows had scarcely bowled a first-class ball between them before the current season, but Elstub had Sutcliffe caught behind down the legside, and Fellows conjured some late swing for Ben Smith to be taken at slip.

Maddy and Habib came together at 28 for 2, and immediately began a purposeful partnership. They saw off the seamers and began tucking in to Ian Fisher, a 24-year-old slow left-arm bowler who trotted up to the wicket like a young pony, lifting his heels in regular motion. It was good to see both batsmen advancing down the wicket to the spinner to lift him over the field. After lunch, when Maddy had reached 50, Habib left the crease again to bring up his own half century with a six.

I was sitting behind two men who had played cricket together some years before. One was in his fifties, but the other - a straight-backed chap with piercing blue eyes, in a very white cap - was 86. "You were a good player, you were, Frank," said his companion. "You'd've got runs in this lot." Given the age difference between them, the octogenarian had presumably played well into middle age. The older man had an extraordinary memory. When his friend speculated about the date of Les Berry's last match, he said immediately: "He was born in 1906".

They were discussing a friend who still played for a Loughborough team. "He's 92," said the younger man. "He's not the oldest bowler in Loughborough," said the octogenarian. "They've got one who's 95."

Not surprisingly, perhaps, age and its consequences was high on their list of topics. The older man was asked if he'd seen "old Ricey" recently, a bowler in their old team whom they both held in high esteem.

"Saw him at Jack's funeral." "Jack? I didn't know he was dead."

"Dropped down dead one morning. I'd only met 'im the week before, too. 'E looked ever so well. Anyway, Ricey was off to another funeral the same day." With sublime good humour, they covered three funerals and a case of terminal cancer in five minutes.

Given the good pitch and the sunny weather, it was the sort of day you would expect Maddy or Habib - or both of them - to go on to a century, but it did not happen. After lunch Silverwood bowled a spell that was noticeably faster and more accurate than his first, and Maddy was caught behind off a dangerous ball that swung away late. Habib followed soon after; once again he was caught in the slips, aiming to force a ball from Silverwood that was too high and too close. Leicestershire were 151 for 4.

As always, Stevens was off and running as soon as his feet hit the ground. The shot of the day was his four through the covers off Silverwood, hit on the up; not far behind it, a lovely glide through mid-wicket. The Australian, Darren Lehmann, captaining Yorkshire in the absence of Byas, wore a flat-brimmed black hat of the kind used by villains in Western films. He obviously believed in bowlers bowling to a field; Hamilton, for instance, ran in to a mere two men on the leg side. Lehmann's field placings for Stevens became more and more extreme. In one over he gave Fellows a deep mid-off, very straight, and two equally straight off-side fielders standing almost side by side a couple of yards in front of the bowler's crease; they were so close they could have held hands.

The overs either side of tea were bad ones for Leicestershire. Wells, after a lively innings of 27, was beaten by a ball from Hamilton that broke back to him; and Stevens fell leg before to the same bowler immediately after the break. A score of 222 for 6 gave the Leicestershire tail yet another chance to show its mettle. Kumble was still in positive mood after his half century at Canterbury, and struck Fisher for six in a lively innings of 19, before charging the same bowler and being stumped. Dakin threw his wicket away, carelessly striking Fisher to deep mid-off.

As at so many first class matches, there were far too many delays in play. The ball change - almost obligatory now - took place after 87 overs. Silverwood twice in succession ran up to the wicket without letting go of the ball - a severe case of memory lapse. Fielding changes continued apace. There was even a moment when silly mid-on and silly mid-off changed places in a playful, circular movement resembling a do-si-do in country dancing. Players may argue that delays are counteracted by the rule requiring a minimum number of overs in the day, but the 104 overs are often a matter of theory rather than practice; today, for instance, bad light obliged the umpires to call play off eight overs early.

Second day

The first hour of the following morning followed a typical Leicestershire course. The opposition would have expected to knock over the last couple of wickets and get on with their innings. Instead, the Leicestershire tail-enders got a breezy 50 or 60 runs to take the total well past 300. Burns played some delightful strokes, well supported by Crowe. The applause for the wicket-keeper's half century confirmed how he had cemented his place in the crowd's affections, in his first season at the club.

A fruitless Yorkshire appeal against Burns drew its automatic response from cheerleader Lewis - a response I had never yet managed to translate. "Back you bedit." "'E's carryin' on again," muttered a member. "'E'll carry on right to the loony bin," said another.

Burns ended his innings (for his part) with a rocketing cut for four off Silverwood; next ball Silverwood ended it (for his part) by knocking out the off stump with a full-length ball. Leicestershire were 351 all out. Silverwood, by far the most impressive of the Yorkshire bowlers, had taken four wickets.

Yorkshire must have the youngest opening pair in county cricket: Victor Craven (aged 20) and Simon Widdup (aged 22). They had added 22 runs when Vince Wells began an inspired spell, wobbling the ball about under an overcast sky. Both Craven and McGrath fell to slip catches by Ben Smith, the second a diving, one-handed effort inches from the ground. When Wells also snared Wood lbw, Yorkshire went in to lunch at 24 for 3.

After lunch the sun came out. Wells kept himself on for a couple of overs, but the magic had gone. There were no complaints: as well as being cricket's enemy, the weather is also responsible for much of its variety. Now Leicestershire's progress was altogether slower. Kumble was tried at the Bennett end, with no joy. Ormond replaced him and had Fellows caught behind from a powerful lifter, but Widdup grafted away, untroubled by very slow scoring. In any case the scoring rate was lifted by the fifth man in, Gavin Hamilton who, when he had made 38, passed Widdup's score. Dakin, Crowe and Kumble were all put to the sword. At length Kumble had Widdup taken at short leg off bat and pad. Yorkshire were 123 for 5.

Ever since the fall of the first Yorkshire wicket spectators had been mystified at the non-appearance of Darren Lehmann, the captain and best batsman. Next morning the daily papers reported that Lehmann had woken with a stiff back and dropped himself down the order, hoping to bat as late as possible. This is just the kind of information spectators would like to know - but how can they? With five wickets down, Lehmann clearly felt he could delay no longer, and emerged pugnaciously from the pavilion. He has a bear-like figure, broad in girth, and sturdy forearms. Despite the back bad, he walked out looking like a man you would entrust with just about any practical task - changing a tyre, for instance, or ejecting a trouble-maker from a bar. Leicestershire cannot have been pleased to see him. At Headingley earlier in the season he had looked immovable, until a lucky run-out disposed of him prematurely.

Once through a torrid first over from Kumble, Lehmann looked as though he was continuing his Headingley innings. The bat came down with arrogant certainty, propelling ground strokes accurately through the field. Boundary followed boundary, eliminating the need for running. He made a special point of taking on Kumble, scoring 12 off one over, and so disorienting the Indian that he bowled one of his no-balls. Lehmann seemed to be playing a different game from everyone else. Seeing him bat, Miranda would have cried again: "Oh brave new world that has such people in it". But there was no secret about the reason for his success: Lehmann was an Australian! He was one of five Aussies in the top 10 batsmen playing English county cricket, all of them with a first-class average between 48 and 55; and none of them good enough for the Australian Test team.

An hour was lost to rain during the afternoon. When play closed, Yorkshire were 194 for 5, with Lehmann on 51 and Hamilton 58.

Third and fourth days

The appeal of the four-day game is its variety. The ebb and flow makes every encounter different, and is in stark contrast to the one-dayers, where most matches follow a similar pattern. Disconcerting, then, that the two Leicestershire/Yorkshire matches in 2000 were so similar in shape. Both saw a full day's play on the first day, a truncated day on the second, and very little play on the last two days. In both, Leicestershire batted first and made a score in the region of 300, with their tail weighing in heavily. In both, the Yorkshire reply began at funereal pace, only to be revived by Lehmann, looking immortal. Neither game offered any real prospect of a result.

At Grace Road the entire third day was washed out, together with the morning of the fourth. At 11.30am on that last day I made a head-count of spectators: 12 men and one woman in the seats around the pavilion area; nine men, one woman and two boys in the pavilion bar; two middle-aged women sitting in front of the shop, with their feet up on the fence; a solitary bloke reading the papers in the covered public seating; and 14 men (one asleep) and two boys in the refreshment room.

This inventory excluded staff, whose numbers probably came close to those of the spectators. Lewis the cheerleader was present in a violet, flowered shirt. Notwithstanding the subdued atmosphere, something amused him, prompting the hyena laugh. This led to a miracle. The elderly man who checked members' passes, and whose face had never shown any expression - let alone amusement - opened his mouth and ejected a series of harsh cries which, I realised, taken together, formed laughter.

As so often happens the morning passed in bright sunshine, with cricket ruled out because of dampness on the wicket. The match was effectively over, and the remaining play, required by regulations, very nearly pointless. To be precise, Yorkshire had three points to play for, and Leicestershire two. The atmosphere was subdued, slightly sad, and... well... pointless. The players must have felt this more than any spectator. A ladder had been placed against their balcony, as though to ensure a quick getaway. Lehmann

121

signed an autograph for a teenage girl in front of the sightscreen. The two teams warmed up on the outfield. One of the Leicestershire players bellowed into a kind of traffic cone: "We're playing pointless cricket."

When play did begin at 2.30pm, the players showed remarkable commitment, given the circumstances. Lehmann saw off James Ormond's opening spell, removed his helmet to don the sherriff's hat, and went remorselessly to his century. Yorkshire were all out for 340 at the close of play. They had secured 10 points from the game, compared to Leicestershire's 11. Surrey, leading the First Division, had had the foresight to win their game in two days before the weather set in, and sat on top of the table with 171 points, followed by Yorkshire with 153, Lancashire with 151 and Leicestershire with 139.

A story told in the refreshment room by an agreeable old member seemed to suit the mood of the day. An old man told his priest he was not at all afraid of dying, but did worry about whether cricket was played in heaven. The next time they met the priest told him: "I checked up on that point for you. The good news is that there is cricket in heaven. The bad news is that you're playing on Saturday week.."

Leicestershire first innings

DL Maddy	c Guy	b Silverwood	66
IJ Sutcliffe	c Guy	b Elstub	2
BF Smith	c McGrath	b Fellows	0
A Habib	c Widdup	b Silverwood	59
DI Stevens	lbw	b Hamilton	49
*VJ Wells		b Hamilton	27
JM Dakin	c Elstub	b Fisher	6
A Kumble	st Guy	b Fisher	19
+ND Burns		b Silverwood	58
CD Crowe		b Silverwood	30
J Ormond	not out		6
Extras			29
Total	All Out		**351**

Bowling	O	M	R	W
Silverwood	25.3	4	60	4
Hamilton	24	2	82	2
Elstub	17	3	44	1
Fellows	17	5	49	1
Fisher	26	2	103	2
Lehmann	1	0	5	0

Yorkshire first innings

S Widdup	c Stevens	b Kumble	38
VJ Craven	c Smith	b Wells	15
A McGrath	c Smith	b Wells	1
MJ Wood	lbw	b Wells	0
GM Fellows	c Burns	b Ormond	16
GM Hamilton		b Ormond	66
*DS Lehmann	c & b Dakin		115
+SM Guy	c Habib	b Dakin	17
ID Fisher	c Habib	b Crowe	24
CEW Silverwood	c Ormond	b Crowe	17
CJ Elstub	not out		2
Extras			29
Total	All Out		340

Bowling	O	M	R	W
Ormond	27	3	82	2
Dakin	19	1	71	2
Wells	12	5	30	3
Kumble	32	9	81	1
Crowe	21.1	4	61	2

Match drawn.
Points: Leicestershire 11, Yorkshire 10

122

14. Leicestershire versus Lancashire
Grace Road, 22 to 25 August

It was instantly apparent to anyone turning up at Grace Road for this match that the ground had received a visitation. Gantries erected on all four sides of the playing area supported unusual constructions, cameras, coils of wire and all the paraphernalia of Sky TV; and out of these constructions came larger-than-life creatures in jackets and ties who - even without make-up - resembled Madame Tussauds models of familiar icons such as Ian Botham and Bob Willis.

The weather for this match was unlike any other during the disastrous summer: all four days ran their course under hot sun, with no loss of play whatsoever. Despite this, and despite the quality of Leicestershire's opposition, and despite, or perhaps because of, the Sky visitation, crowds were disappointingly thin throughout.

The cricket was different too. The clatter of wickets in two-and-a-half day matches had become so common that it was strange to see a game extending over four full days of play. The phrase "grown up cricket" was used on Sky by Bob Willis, a pundit whose seemingly bored-rigid demeanour on air masks a highly informative commentary, with a dry sense of humour.

Ben Smith, substituting as captain for the injured Vince Wells, won the toss for Leicestershire and decided to bat. Sutcliffe and Smith both fell quickly, but Maddy looked in very good shape until he fell to the first of two superb catches taken in this innings. A violent, downward hook had everyone looking to the boundary, but Chilton - fielding quite close to the bat at square leg - flung himself down to take the ball two-handed, just inches from the ground. When Stevens fell second ball to a slip catch, Leicestershire had reached a familiar-looking score of 70 for 4 - and this on a pitch which, everyone agreed, was a belter for batting.

The presence of TV cameras may or may not alter the behaviour patterns of players, but it certainly changes the habits of spectators. Lewis the cheerleader, always prominent, was positively 'in yer face' with his vocal pyrotechnics on this first broadcast day. Wearing a conical straw hat on top of a violently coloured shirt he looked like an extra from '*The King and I*', and clashed with a man standing next to him who was wearing a red and white striped shirt, in his case resembling a stick of Brighton rock.

The pairing of Habib and Dakin is perhaps Leicestershire's most productive, and most interesting to watch, and their stand extended well beyond the lunch interval. Habib is almost a banker for at least one half century per match, which is just as well given the persistent failure of the top order, and Dakin played one of his responsible innings, full of restrained ground strokes.

Dakin eventually fell caught at slip when he misread a googly from Chris Schofield - the leg-spinner awarded an England team contract at the beginning of the season. Despite fulfilling the quota of bad balls expected of his breed, Schofield's bowling in this match boded well for English cricket in the future. Looking absurdly young (which he is), he bowled with shirt flapping out at the back, as if called unexpectedly out of bed to perform in a night shirt. He ambles towards the wicket, then, as though trying to take the batsman by surprise, bursts into a flurry of arms and legs and tosses the ball down quite rapidly, extracting considerable spin - even halfway through the first day.

The Grace Road public address system had gone haywire for the past two matches, and two seventy-ish members behind me broke off from a deep conversation to query an inaudible announcement.

"Did you 'ear that, Nev?"

"Yes."

"What did 'e say?"

"Dunno. I 'eard it, but I could'nt 'ear what 'e said."

They resumed their conversation, of which James Joyce would have been proud. Before I moved away to the tea-room they had covered Bradman, great Lancashire teams of the past, the prospects of Harry Pilling as a jockey, a Russian submarine disaster, the wearing of medals at local government ceremonies and the dangers of swimming out to sea.

Philip DeFreitas, back in the Leicestershire side after injury, joined Habib and immediately played like a top order batsman, as he had all season. Together they took the score to 242 for 5 at tea, with Habib on 77 and DeFreitas on 42. By this time Lancashire had used eight bowlers: the opening pair, Chapple and Smethurst, the spinners, Schofield and Keedy, plus Flintoff, Ganguly, Fairbrother and Chilton. The most interesting of these was Mike Smethurst, a 23-year-old quickie who, before this season, had played a mere five first class matches, then established himself in the side following a long-term injury to Peter Martin - the cricket equivalent of stepping in from the chorus line. He already had 35 wickets at 25 apiece during the season. A longish run-in, side-on delivery and big final leap make him decidedly quick, and a height of six foot five inches gives him plenty of bounce on most wickets, though not on this Grace Road one.

Habib and DeFreitas took 12 off a Chapple over, the latter reaching a half century in only 67 balls. On this pitch, patience was required from both bowlers and fielders. Flintoff, the solitary slip, rested between overs by leaning on a tolerant wicket-keeper Hegg, who must have felt there was a small hillside on top of him. Habib had reached 93 with a flurry of boundaries when he was wonderfully well caught when lashing out at a short ball from Schofield. Mike Atherton turned at mid-wicket, ran 25 yards full pelt towards the boundary, and took the ball two-handed, while falling. As ever, all this was done undemonstratively. His feat meant that Habib had missed out on a century. "Does it soften the blow?" mused a spectator, "falling to a catch like that?"

DeFreitas was entirely unabashed by wickets falling at the other end, and shortly before the close of play brought his score to 90 with a straight six off Keedy - and every prospect of a century the next morning. As he walked off, Lewis the cheerleader ran onto the pitch to take an arm, on camera.

Second day

Leicestershire began the second day on 362 for 7, and within a quarter of an hour were 372 all out, DeFreitas scoring 97. Chapple and Schofield had three wickets each, and Smethurst two. Was 372 a good score? The Sky pundits were uncertain. They felt that the pitch would deteriorate and take spin, and that Leicestershire may have done enough to give their opponents an awkward fourth innings - with two spinners, Kumble and Crowe, playing in their side.

On paper the Lancashire batting order looked formidable - certainly the strongest in English county cricket. Atherton and Mark Chilton put on 50 at four an over, a rate which was not matched for the rest of their team's innings. When Chilton fell, John Crawley hit the first ball he received straight for four, and looked in tremendously good form. Throughout the afternoon, first with Atherton and then with Flintoff, he put the Leicestershire attack to the sword. Seeing him bat, it seemed remarkable that he had played only 27 times for England - the same number as Mark

Butcher, and far fewer than Mark Ramprakash or Graham Hick. His first class average of 48 was the highest of all English players with the exception of Hick. He has a very well organised defence, his reach on the forward defensive stroke suggesting the illegal use of telescopic wrists. Crawley is one of those players who without fuss can turn good line and length balls to the mid-wicket boundary, and in doing so generate an almost inaudible kiss of willow on leather - of a sort which for most players indicates a snick to the wicket-keeper. There were several of these strokes in his first 50, which came after a mere 72 balls.

Atherton's departure for 48, trapped by a DeFreitas ball which kept low, merely presaged the entrance of another England batsman. In a brisk innings, Andrew Flintoff struck a number of powerful blows, including a straight six off the spinner Crowe. The only light relief for Leicestershire came when the umpire called "Whoa" as his hat blew off and bowled down the pitch, just as DeFreitas ran in. At tea Lancashire were 219 for 2, with Crawley on 92 and Flintoff 34.

There was never a point at which the Lancashire batsmen cut loose; they simply accumulated runs remorselessly. The slow torture continued after the break. Just after 5pm Flintoff reached his 50 with 12 in an over from Dakin, but was then caught by silly mid-off from Kumble's bowling. The sight of his replacement - the world-class Indian batsman Saurav Ganguly - would not have raised Leicestershire's spirits, and the run glut was only checked when Ganguly disappeared back into the pavilion for a while, causing a lengthy, unexplained delay.

The presence of the Sky team provided some interesting contrasts between watching on screen *vis-a-vis* in the flesh. From time to time a spectator would return with additional information gleaned from the TV screens in the pavilion bar, illuminating some aspect of play which could not be interpreted from beyond the boundary boards. For instance, Ganguly had gone off to have his contact lenses attended to and, the commentators felt, should have been kept off by the umpires until another wicket fell. Similarly, Flintoff's dismissal was confirmed as a bat/pad decision. Even Sky commentators cannot know everything, though. There was a moment when a production minion came to the edge of the boundary, cameras presumably averted, to enquire about some detail from Smethurst; the player ran across to ask his captain, then relayed the information, which was no doubt soon passed on to viewers by the omniscient Sky commentary team.

During this rather scrappy period of play, John Dakin tested his credentials to enter a 'world's strongest man' competition: first he shifted a couple of heavy, wheeled pieces of cover equipment single-handed, when the ball ran under them from a boundary stroke; then demonstrated his prodigious throw by returning the ball over the stumps from the boundary edge from a kneeling position. How about a wrestling bout, Sumo style, between Dakin and his fellow giant, Andrew Flintoff?

Lancashire ground on remorselessly. Crawley's excellent century came from 187 balls, and contained 15 boundaries: of these, six were directed to the mid-wicket area, another two to square leg, and one to fine leg. Ganguly accumulated chancelessly. Leicestershire's difficulties were enhanced by injury: Ormond had twice left the field with a hamstring problem, and DeFreitas pulled up in the afternoon session with a twisted knee. Their team's plight was highlighted by the sight of Chris Lewis gliding into the ground in a large, open-top car just before the close of play, and sauntering, designer-clothed, into the pavilion. At the close, Lancashire were 334 for 3, with Crawley on 129 and Ganguly 42. It was ominous.

Third day

I decided to watch the third day of the match at home on a Sky channel, to compare the experience with that of 'being there'. As things turned out, this was an extraordinary day of county cricket, reminiscent of cricket in the 1940s rather than the year 2000. Both captains took a clear tactical line, and adhered to it with great determination. Crawley wanted Lancashire to bat for most of the day and grind out an enormous score, so that he could bowl out the opposition on a wearing pitch. He was aided in this by Leicestershire's injuries. Of the five main bowlers, all three seamers had problems: Dakin with an Achilles tendon, Ormond with his damaged hamstring, and DeFreitas with his twisted knee. In the circumstances the two spinners might be expected to shoulder the main burden, but Crowe was sent home at the start of play with *sunstroke*; and Kumble had bowled poorly and expensively.

Ben Smith now showed what a thoughtful captain he could be, given the opportunity. Leicestershire were entitled to take the new ball at the start of play, but they declined. The cull of their seamers was obviously a factor, but they also wanted to restrict Lancashire's scoring by sticking to the old, worn ball, which came off the bat much more slowly. Smith's main instrument of control was DeFreitas, who came on at the start of play, switched from medium pace to fast off-spin at 11.30am, with Kumble helping him to set his field, and bowled unchanged until just before lunch - all this with a dodgy knee. On the whole the tactics were vindicated, for Lancashire were restricted to 101 runs in the morning session, giving them a lead of only 63. Crawley cut Dakin to Stevens at point when he had made 139, to be replaced by Fairbrother, playing more soberly than was his custom. Ganguly, after a very slow start, accelerated to 86 by the interval. Ormond was back on the field, but because of previous absences could not bowl until just before lunch; when he did, eventually, replace DeFreitas he too bowled slow off-breaks. It was all very strange.

After lunch Ormond briefly switched to quick mode and surprised Ganguly, lbw for 87. It made little difference to the Lancashire innings. Hegg came to the wicket and, with Fairbrother, continued the procession of large, attritional partnerships; up to the fall of Ganguly's wicket these had amounted to 59, 97, 89, 107, and 84. For a side with one fit bowler, and three half-fit, these scores were depressing, to say the least. If Lancashire felt any sympathy it was not expressed on the field of play, but the scoring, though remorseless, never got out of hand. That much was signified by Fairbrother's 50, which took 134 balls, and contained only five boundaries.

For a spectator from Leicestershire, the spectacle generated horrified fascination rather than enjoyment. Lancashire's purpose was not to entertain but to win the game, and join Surrey at the top of the championship table. As they ground on throughout the afternoon, DeFreitas came back for another spell, beginning his 42nd over. The Leicestershire fielders - and what was left of the bowlers - kept up their spirits admirably, and there were no easy runs through the field. Umpire Alan Whitehead became the latest casualty, retiring with a hurt foot, to be replaced by the third umpire. Fairbrother and Hegg posted a 100 partnership, and after tea Fairbrother reached his century. Crawley declared with his total on a massive 574 for 5 with Hegg not out on 65. There had been 59 extras. DeFreitas, with a wrenched knee, had bowled 47 overs and taken 2 for 112. Guts apart, the quality of his performance was shown by the contrasting figures of Leicestershire's main spin bowler, on a wicket suited to spin: Kumble had 1 for 140 from 45 overs.

The most bizarre feature of a highly unusual day was that Leicestershire bowled 177 overs with one ball. By the close, the seam had almost entirely worn away. This was almost the first match of Leicestershire's season when the ball had not needed changing before 100 overs because it was out of shape. How fortunate then that there was no call for a replacement ball at 150 overs, because one would surely not have been available. The proof of Leicestershire's tactics would only be known at the end of the match, but Ben Smith could already claim some profit from them: despite posting a score of nearly 600, and having five wickets in hand, Lancashire had not exceeded a scoring rate of 3.2 an over.

In the hour and a half of play that remained on the third day, Leicestershire took their score to 75 for 1. Sutcliffe, the main contributor, was on 44 not out at the close.

It was interesting to compare a day spent seated before the television screen with the two preceding days at the ground itself. Both modes of watching had their advantages. Viewing on Sky obviously gave a much clearer sight than even the most powerful pair of binoculars of what precisely happened in the key wicket-to-wicket area - notably the amount of spin and movement exacted by the bowler, and the batsman's reaction to it. This was observable for balls bowled at both ends of the pitch, something clearly ruled out for spectators at the ground. Of course, any incident arousing interest, or doubt, could immediately be replayed in slow motion - a feature denied to on-the-spot onlookers, who must learn the art of close, sustained observation if they are not to miss much of the action.

Minute detail such as the facial expression of participants is another advantage of screen viewing. For instance in the first few minutes of play, spectators at the ground would have seen John Crawley pull back from the wicket as the bowler was about to deliver, but would not have known why; Sky viewers had a clear view of the wasp buzzing inside his helmet.

The other obvious advantage of Sky viewing is access to a team of commentators who know what they are talking about and can express themselves with conviction. The downside to this - that it pre-empts spectators from thinking for themselves - detracts even further if the commentators get it wrong. At the end of the fourth day the early predictions of a crumbling pitch remained unfulfilled.

Of course, there are also strong advantages to being at the match itself - which is just as well, because most county cricket games are not televised. What I missed most was the atmosphere and camaraderie, and the opportunity to air rumour and gossip which was too scandalous for Sky commentators to risk. Spectators can walk around the ground to determine their own preferred viewpoints, though this is partly provided for by new Sky digital technology giving viewers some control over camera angles. Also, at the ground, details of the match are readily available from the scoreboard at any time, though again the new technology provides a service that is almost as good in this respect. Finally, 'real' spectators at the ground see the whole picture all the time. This is not quite as important as, for instance, at a football match, but it would have permitted Stevens's catch off John Crawley to be followed from the bat - whereas the Sky cameras missed it first time around.

Fourth day

At the beginning of the fourth day this Grace Road match seemed, like the Yorkshire match before it, to be repeating early season history. In early May, the game at Old Trafford saw Leicestershire bat first and make an inadequate total of 265. Lancashire had replied massively, with a score including two centuries (Fairbrother again, and Flintoff), and then bowled Leicestershire out for an innings victory. Was it to happen again? Lancashire had a lead of 202 from the first innings, and a whole day to bowl out their opponents and knock off the winning runs, if this was required. To salvage a draw, Leicestershire would need to bat until after tea. It was in their favour that the first innings deficit was not out of sight completely, so that making runs would be a constructive activity. On the other hand, five hours is a long time to survive on a wearing pitch.

By lunch, at 169 for 4, the odds were firmly on a Lancashire win. Sutcliffe went past his half century, but was caught at deep mid-wicket from a mistimed sweep off Keedy. Ben Smith was approaching his own half century when he snicked Schofield to slip. Stevens scored some quick runs, but was taken at silly mid on off Keedy. These were classic spinning dismissals. And also classic Leicestershire top order batting, with players making a contribution, but not going on. Notwithstanding these events, the pitch was taking only moderate spin. Crawley gave the lion's share of the bowling to his two twirlers, switching them round from time to time, and occasionally inserting a few overs of variety from one of the quicker men. From one of these spells Flintoff was at his worst, generating four wides, four leg byes and a no ball in a two-over stint.

Aftab Habib, 28 not out at lunch, was the one Leicestershire batsman to build an innings from a base of solid defence. For a while, Dakin's enormous reach allowed him to disturb the boundary ropes with surprisingly gentle, almost caressing strokes, but he too fell to a close fielder in front of the stumps, from a Schofield leg break which zipped off the wicket. Leicestershire were 195 for 5, still seven runs behind, with 56 overs left.

Enter Philip DeFreitas. After all he had done already Leicestershire had no right to expect a further contribution. Immediately, he skied a drive to long off; Smethurst, fielding at deep mid off, chased after it, but misjudged the flight as completely as Atherton had judged his first innings catch, and the ball thudded harmlessly to earth. At 202, Leicestershire's score passed 'into the black', so that every run scored meant one Lancashire had to score in turn during their fourth innings. From now on, spectators of both sides kept an eye on the 'overs remaining' column of the scoreboard as it ticked down, too slowly for Leicestershire supporters, and far too quickly for those of Lancashire.

Daffy celebrated his reprieve with three boundaries off bad balls from Schofield: a cut and a cover drive from short deliveries, and a straight drive from a full toss. A fourth boundary off Keedy was unintended, as a snick in the air eluded both wicket-keeper and slip. Perhaps this miss marked the turning point of the day. Leicestershire were 237 for 5, with 44 overs left.

A single took Habib to his 50, made from 140 balls, after nearly three hours at the crease. It seemed that almost every Leicestershire innings was now built around him. He was very nearly run out going for an impossible single, of the sort that no batsman can rationalise after the event. It was all too much for a Lancashire supporter, one of a number in the crowd, with a glass of wine in hand, feet up on the seats in front, sporting a pair of custard-yellow socks. He shouted: "Come on, Lancashire. Go for the throat."

The stand continued, each boundary a blow to Lancashire's ambitions. DeFreitas struck Ganguly through the covers, and the batsmen took 13 off an over from Schofield: a back foot cover drive from Habib, and a cover drive and sweep from DeFreitas. "Come on the red rose."

Shortly before tea DeFreitas reached his second half century of the match. It had taken 84 balls, and by accelerating the run rate had complemented Habib's contribution perfectly. The two had been easily Leicestershire's biggest scorers of the season. The importance of their stand was shown by yellow socks's regular interjections: "Boring, boring, Leicestershire."

Tea was taken at 290 for 5, with Habib on 71 and DeFreitas 50. Leicestershire were 88 ahead with 27 overs remaining. Afterwards, Habib fell to Keedy for 73, again a slip catch after a resumption, having put on 111 with DeFreitas. The flicker of optimism felt by Lancashire supporters was soon extinguished by Burns, batting with great good sense and not a few strokes. The 'equation', a word increasingly used by sports commentators with no regard to its mathematical connotations, between overs left and runs required by Lancashire was entering the realms of fantasy.

"Boring, *boring*, Leicestershire."

It happened that as 5pm approached, Burns dominated the strike for a while, and there seemed nothing left in the game but quietly to play out time. Then DeFreitas got down to the action end, pulled Smethurst for four, sent Schofield to the long on boundary, and took eight runs past the wicket-keeper from two mistimed acts of violence. Suddenly he was on 91, and his demeanour clearly indicated that he was going for a century. He hooked Smethurst to the boundary, took two from a massive hoick to long on, and smashed Schofield to mid-wicket to reach 102 from 135 balls, with 18 fours. Even then there was energy left, from some deep reserve unknown to most mortals. When John Crawley signalled surrender by bowling an over himself, Daffy struck him for three sixes in succession. One of these was nearly caught by a spectator and Mike Atherton, trotting over to retrieve it, gave him some genial advice on technique.

Daffy finished on 123 not out, following 97 in the first innings, and bowling 47 overs in Lancashire's marathon innings. Few players can have made such a contribution to a first class game. And the man was 34 years of age! He had nothing left to prove, except to live up to broadcaster Christopher Martin-Jenkins's charming description of him, earlier in the season, as "a national treasure".

Leicestershire's final score of 408 for 6 disguised how closely they came to losing this match, and how closely Lancashire came to winning it, and topping the championship table. Amid the sheer, grinding business of run-scoring in this form of 'grown up' cricket, there were numerous points of interest, including Crawley's batting, Schofield's bowling and the monumental performance of DeFreitas. Leicestershire's fielding held up very well against the physical collapse of almost their entire bowling squad. On this pitch, tactics ultimately decided the result: Lancashire's failure to raise the scoring rate in their mammoth innings, and so give themselves time to bowl the opposition out; and Ben Smith's bloody-minded decision to bowl 170 overs with the same ball.

The game left Lancashire in second place in the table with 163 points from 14 games, to Surrey's 171 from 13 games. Yorkshire were third with 153 (13 games), and Leicestershire fourth with 148 (14 games). These four were all out of reach of the fifth-placed side.

Leicestershire first innings

DL Maddy	c Chilton b Flintoff		26
IJ Sutcliffe	lbw	b Chapple	7
*BF Smith	c Chilton b Smethurst		10
A Habib	c Atherton b Schofield		93
DI Stevens	c Fairbrother b Flintoff		0
JM Dakin	c Ganguly b Schofield		50
PAJ DeFreitas		b Smethurst	97
+ND Burns		b Schofield	15
A Kumble		b Chapple	28
CD Crowe	not out		0
J Ormond		b Chapple	0
Extras			46
Total	All Out		**372**

Bowling	O	M	R	W
Chapple	19	4	54	3
Smethurst	21	3	72	2
Flintoff	13	3	43	2
Ganguly	9	1	45	0
Keedy	16	3	49	0
Schofield	27	3	78	3
Chilton	1	0	3	0
Fairbrother	3	1	6	0

Lancashire first innings

MA Atherton	lbw	b DeFreitas	48
MJ Chilton		b DeFreitas	21
*JP Crawley	c Stevens b Dakin		139
A Flintoff	c Sutcliffe b Kumble		55
SC Ganguly	lbw	b Ormond	87
NH Fairbrother	not out		100
+WK Hegg	not out		65
Extras			59
Total	5 wickets declared		**574**

Bowling	O	M	R	W
Ormond	29	3	76	1
Dakin	30	2	112	1
DeFreitas	47	7	112	2
Kumble	45	9	140	1
Crowe	20	2	74	0
Maddy	6	1	21	0

Leicestershire second innings

DL Maddy	c Hegg	b Schofield	9
IJ Sutcliffe	c Chapple b Keedy		52
*BF Smith	c Ganguly b Schofield		44
A Habib	c Ganguly b Keedy		73
DI Stevens	c Chilton b Keedy		16
JM Dakin	c Flintoff b Schofield		18
PAJ DeFreitas	not out		123
+ND Burns	not out		30
Extras			43
Total	6 wickets		**408**

Bowling	O	M	R	W
Chapple	20	1	89	0
Smethurst	9	2	32	0
Schofield	43	8	149	3
Keedy	34	7	77	3
Flintoff	2	0	9	0
Ganguly	3	0	8	0
Crawley	1	0	19	0

Match drawn. Points: Lancashire 12, Leicestershire 9

Taunton:
Top: looking towards the town centre. (Photo: John Holland)
Bottom: Waiting for the rain to stop (Photo: John Holland)

15. Somerset versus Leicestershire
Taunton, 1 to 4 September

All too many of Leicestershire's matches were spoiled by the weather in 2000, but this was the first to be ruined from day one. The loss of the first four sessions on a very good batting pitch rendered a draw inevitable from the outset.

Well... not quite all of four sessions. In the mid-afternoon of the first day I got into the ground - of which more later - to check on the prospects of play. It seemed highly unlikely. A lot of rain had fallen, and the sky was clearly about to unload more. A mere handful of spectators were in the stands. I retired to one of the toilets, where I heard - to my amazement - the announcement: "From the pavilion end, Philip DeFreitas". Shortly afterwards there was a ragged cheer, and I emerged to see the players coming off for rain. Three balls had been bowled, with the hapless Mark Lathwell caught behind off one of them. Play was over until the following day.

Two middle-aged men passed me, making for the exit. "That's it, then," said one, without irony. "I really enjoyed the day."

More rain fell during the night and it was 1.30pm before play began on the second day, under a blue sky, on an extremely damp pitch. Not surprisingly, only a few hundred spectators were there to see it. The place had an end-of-season air, like a seaside pier after the schools had gone back. I had arrived at 12.30pm and, as on the preceding day, passed through gates denuded of attendants, quite unable to find anyone to take my money; Taunton's defences were down.

The ground had a pleasing homeliness; the river Tone ran along one side (repository of numerous sixes during the Botham/Richards era), and another perimeter was overlooked by the tower of St James' church. Most striking was the small size of the playing area. Both straight boundaries were short, and one of the square boundaries allowed spectators closer to the play than I had been all season.

There were places where homeliness gave way to tackiness. The sightscreens, for instance. "I think they're horrible," said a woman member, with feeling. At one end they comprised some grubby white sheets fixed to uprights, resembling the rigging of a rudimentary sailing vessel; at the other, white sheets were simply draped down the length of the stands, in most unsightly fashion. At one corner of the ground was the most extraordinary stand I had seen all year: a covered affair containing an array of deep, padded seats of different colours - red, blue, green, yellow and, in one case, red with yellow arms. The stand faced out, at the wrong angle, onto an empty stretch of the playing area; its inhabitants sat there, far distant from the play, like travellers in the departure lounge of a long-abandoned airport.

That early wicket in the first three balls had been an anomaly and Somerset settled down to build a large score, aided by a batters' surface and the short boundaries. The county had recorded more batting points than any side in the first division bar Leicestershire, and the points on offer in this match could shore them up against the prospect, remote, but still possible, of relegation. For Leicestershire, there was little to play for except pride. Cox, Turner and Parsons all contributed scores of 40 and over and Somerset finished the day on 273 for 6.

Under the circumstances of semi-pointless cricket, spectators must look elsewhere for entertainment. The afternoon session saw an extraordinary sequence of Leicestershire players going off the field for minor stresses and strains, and coming back on again - so much so that a spectator shouted: "They think it's a game of musical chairs". Ben Smith was one to go off but, when Vince Wells also retired, Smith was obliged to return. Coming through the pavilion gate he tripped over a trailing bootlace, fell full length on the outfield, and stayed down. "He'll go off again now," cried the wag. DeFreitas, just preparing to bowl, and one of the few players to notice Smith's brilliant piece of comic timing, was unable to go on; he lay down near his bowling mark, giggling uncontrollably.

As 6pm approached, one could see why September's county cricket matches start at 10.30am rather than the customary 11.00am. Deprived of the sun, the ground darkened abruptly; a wintry chill signalled that the summer game was nearly over for another year.

Third day

The ideal for a visiting supporter is to find accommodation with cricketing connections. Breakfast at the very pleasant Ford House in Taunton was enhanced by meandering cricket talk with both the landlord and his wife.

The third day began promptly, at the earlier time, chimed in by the bells of St James' church. I long to put a second 's' after the apostrophe, but have recorded the name just as it was on the church sign. With only batting points and perhaps a few for bowling in prospect, batsmen on both sides prepared to fill their boots. Prominent among these for the home team was the 22-year-old Somerset all-rounder, Ian Blackwell. He cuts an extraordinary figure. To say that he was constructed like the proverbial brick outhouse might cause the architect to sue. Blackwell's 15-stone figure, surmounted by blond rinsed hair, is of Flintoffian or Dakinesque proportions - and, as with those two heavyweights, when he hits the ball it stays hit. He pounded the Leicestershire bowlers all over the ground, reaching a maiden, and very warmly applauded, century off only 129 balls.

Bonus points were Somerset's objective, and they declared their innings shortly after reaching the fifth batting point, at 411 for 6. Of these runs, all of 64 came from extras, after an epidemic of no-balls affecting all the bowlers except Wells. One interminable over from Boswell included two wides and a no-ball, as well as seven runs from the bat - one of those cases where a reliable bowler temporarily goes haywire for no apparent reason.

Fourth day

How bowlers must sigh at the prospect of Taunton. Somerset members around the ground were already predicting a large Leicestershire score, and they were not wrong. Darren Maddy recorded his first century of the season, and several other batsmen tucked in. The match ended on the fourth day with Leicestershire all out for 470, and Somerset 90 for 2 in their second innings.

Throughout the season the national press had been blaming poor county pitches for the state of batting in the English game. The Taunton ground produces good strips, of the kind which catapulted Marcus Trescothick into the England side, but then Somerset have not won a four-day game there all season - nor lost one. As I left the ground an agreeable Somerset member, a man in his seventies, was daring to give voice to doubts. "I think - you'll probably all shoot me, now," he said to his companions "that these wickets are too easy paced."

As the Taunton game stuttered to a close, the England team were involved in a thrilling match at the Oval, wrapping up their first series win over the West Indies for 31 years - with Somerset's Andrew Caddick and Marcus Trescothick both prominent in the action. Not least among the reasons for England's victory was the feather-bedding of players through the 'central contracts' system, which had resulted - most unusually - in the main strike force of Gough and Caddick remaining fit throughout the summer's seven Test matches. There was a downside to this for Somerset members: the absence of Caddick and Trescothick from their team for most of the season.

"If we can have a strong England *and* a strong Somerset, all well and good..." a Taunton member was saying to a friend, at the close. And if not? No need to spell out the corollary. This man - blazered, opinionated, stuffed with local pride - was a reminder of the reactionary county establishment that the ECB had to win over if they were to continue their resuscitation of the national game.

Somerset first innings

					Bowling	O	M	R	W
MN Lathwell	c Burns	b DeFreitas	0		DeFreitas	25	4	81	2
*J Cox	lbw	b DeFreitas	58		Boswell	17	3	64	2
+RJ Turner	lbw	b Kumble	47		Dakin	14	2	59	0
KA Parsons	c Sutcliffe	b Kumble	48		Kumble	34	5	117	2
M Burns	c Burns	b Boswell	23		Wells	7	0	40	0
GD Rose	c Burns	b Boswell	5		Maddy	6	0	34	1
ID Blackwell	c Habib	b Maddy	109						
PD Bowler	not out		38						
JID Kerr	not out		19						
Extras			64						
Total	7 wickets declared		**411**						

Leicestershire first innings

					Bowling	O	M	R	W
DL Maddy	lbw	b Grove	102		Rose	25	4	69	1
IJ Sutcliffe	lbw	b Jones	1		Jones	28	5	116	2
BF Smith	c Cox	b Rose	69		Kerr	23	3	97	4
A Habib	lbw	b Kerr	72		Grove	18	3	72	1
DI Stevens	c Turner	b Kerr	0		Blackwell	21	4	78	1
*VJ Wells	c Jones	b Kerr	98		Burns	7.2	0	28	1
JM Dakin		b Blackwell	16						
PAJ DeFreitas	c Turner	b Kerr	0						
+ND Burns	c Turner	b Jones	57						
A Kumble	c Bowler	b Burns	35						
SAJ Boswell	not out		0						
Extras			20						
Total	All Out		**470**						

Somerset second innings

					Bowling	O	M	R	W
*J Cox	not out		40		DeFreitas	8	1	24	1
MN Lathwell	c Maddy	b Boswell	7		Boswell	6	0	18	1
+RJ Turner	c Burns	b DeFreitas	3		Maddy	6	1	15	0
PD Bowler	not out		27		Wells	4	1	20	0
Extras			13		Smith	2	0	6	0
Total	2 wickets		**90**		Stevens	1	0	6	0

Match drawn. Points: Somerset 8, Leicestershire 7

16. Leicestershire versus Kent
Grace Road, 13 to 16 September

Leicestershire's last four-day game of the season was against Kent, at Grace Road in mid-September. The upshot was a fitting - if depressing - reflection of the season as a whole: a single day's play, followed by three whole days washed out in a torrent of rain. Kent did not even have time to complete one innings, registering 228 for 8 in the six hours available. It was a suitable full stop to a season which made even the most fanatical cricket supporter query whether the English climate was suited to the game.

At the beginning of that first session I found a single person sitting in the covered stands along the side of the playing area - a woman in her fifties, of ample figure and friendly disposition. When I said that we had the stand to ourselves, she observed that she would be moving on at 11am, to start work for the caterers who operated in the main restaurant.

"Must be difficult working when you're also a cricket fan," I said. "Your attention must wander." "No, I don't know about the game," she replied. "I've worked here for years and I can't make head nor tail of it. All those numbers up there..." She glanced up at the main score-board. "If you offered me £1,000 I couldn't tell you what they mean. It's all too complicated." She sounded quite put out. "I can't even tell you who's winning at the moment..."

"Well, they've only been playing half an hour," I said. "You can't say either side is winning so early in the game."

"Oh well, I don't know." She pointed to the boundary rope in front of us. "What's that string doing there?" Here was an easy one to start with, I thought. "It's the boundary rope. It's to signify the edge of the playing area." She responded: "I thought it might be to stop the ball going across." "No, it means that if the ball crosses the rope, the batsmen get four runs." "Oh." She was looking uncertain. "Except... if it goes across without bouncing, they get six."

"You see what I mean," she cried, getting flustered again, and throwing her arms up. "It's hopeless. I'll never understand it."

I had to sympathise. Once you stop to analyse, it gets complicated. Not many would agree with Nasser Hussain's recent statement that "cricket was a simple game".

This was an old-fashioned match, in that there was nothing to play for except the game itself. Kent needed, and soon secured, a single point to stay in the first division. Leicestershire were already safe from relegation but out of contention for the champion and runners-up slots. Add to this the gloomy weather forecast, which made it pretty clear that the match would not finish, and the players' commitment throughout the first day was commendable.

From a batting point of view, Raul Dravid's innings was the main attraction. As in the Canterbury match between the teams, he started off like a train, became more sedate, then got out, for 77 in this case, when he should have reached 100.

From a bowling perspective the performance of Billy Stelling in his first four-day match for Leicestershire was a major surprise. He came on just after mid-day and bowled a maiden. "That was quite a decent over," said the man in front of me to his companion. Stelling followed this with another 24 'decent' overs, had two catches dropped off him, and still finished with 5 for 49. Leicestershire had been short of a quick bowler all season. All over the ground member was turning to member and exclaiming "Why haven't we played this man before?"

Unusually, all eight wickets that fell on the day were caught by Burns the wicket-keeper (five) or in the slips.

I walked round the ground for - as it turned out - the last time that year. A small crowd had turned up to view the last rites, and one could almost see the season grinding to a halt - along with Kent's run rate, which fell from nearly three an over at lunch to less than 2.5 by the close. A party of school children, in red uniforms, gave much needed colour to the stands. The chill of winter was in the air. Under heavy cloud, the atmosphere was subdued, and shouts from the fielders could be heard across the ground. Soon the whole area would lie undisturbed throughout the winter months.

Kent first innings

DP Fulton	c Wells	b Ormond	16
JB Hockley	c Burns	b Ormond	2
R Dravid	c Burns	b Stelling	77
ET Smith	c Maddy	b Stelling	40
MJ Walker	c Burns	b Wells	19
*MA Ealham	c Maddy	b Stelling	19
+PA Nixon	not out		29
MJ McCague	c Burns	b Stelling	3
MJ Saggers	c Burns	b Stelling	6
DA Scott	not out		2
Extras			15
Total	8 wickets		**228**

Bowling	O	M	R	W
Ormond	27	2	91	2
DeFreitas	20	4	46	0
Wells	16	5	28	1
Stelling	25	8	49	5
Maddy	4	1	7	0

Match drawn.
Points: Leicestershire 6, Kent 5

Conclusion: County Cricket 2000

I had set out at the beginning of the season to watch all of Leicestershire's four-day matches. In the event I missed three days - outside those destroyed by bad weather.

Of the 16 games I watched, eight were so badly treated by the weather that draws became almost inevitable Some of these climatic problems could be avoided. The distribution of fixtures in the calendar was wilfully strange. Leicestershire had six four-day matches before the end of May (four of which were rain-ruined), just one in the relatively placid month of June, and two in September (both rain-ruined).

I was visiting all the grounds for the first time. One eye-opener was the determination of cricket managements to keep their grounds a secret from the public. At several locations the first-time visitor had to locate the entrance via a narrow, unsignposted track, at the end of which sat a white-coated attendant with a tin box, to receive the admission money. "This is our little secret, this is," said one of them. The absence of sign posting sent out distinct messages: If you do not know where the ground is, you should do; this is a club, for members, and we do not believe in sordid advertising, or self-promotion. There was almost a hint of the gentleman's club ethos - do not approach us; we will approach you.

Members' facilities do resemble those of a gentleman's club - a second home (at least in the summer), friends and acquaintances to talk to (though not necessarily to be tied down to), food and drink - with the addition of something to do (watch cricket). Unlike gentleman's clubs, the cricket clubs do not exclude women, who often accompany their husbands, especially if they can knit, and sometimes even join on their own account.

That said, the pleasure of excluding others remains part of the scene. The 'gentlemen versus players' aspect of cricket has gone from the playing area, but remains in the stands.

Members can enjoy the best of the facilities, and see non-members (including the away non-members) relegated to crude seating enclosures, distant from the action and uncovered.

Catering arrangements, sometimes quite lavish and varied for members, are often vestigial for non-members; I can scarcely believe, even now, that I could not find a sandwich at Headingley or Old Trafford. In fact, county cricket clubs are obsessed with their existing membership. It is almost as if facilities for the casual spectator are deliberately downgraded, so that membership is seen as the only option - even though those who pay at the gate pay, comparatively, through the nose. On top of this, all sorts of exclusive arrangements are to be found, a tent for 'committee members' here, an enclosure for 'vice-presidents' there, and so on. Cricket remains a distinctly status-conscious environment.

Not surprisingly, the majority of spectators seen at county games are oldsters, or young children brought by oldsters. Of course there is a good reason for attendance to be dominated by the old: they have the time. But from the clubs' point of view there is an obvious reason for targeting the 20-55 year-old group: they become old. Where are members of the future to come from? People are hardly likely to pile in with membership applications at 60 unless they have previously attended, and enjoyed cricket. For a 30-year old, watching cricket amid a band, as it must seem, of sheltered housing inhabitants cannot be much of a turn-on.

Least of all do the clubs target young members. True, young children (and old) are allowed to play on the outfield during intervals - an agreeable custom. But few of the extra activities arranged by clubs for spectators (for instance, a "ladies' hat day" at Canterbury) stand a cat's chance in hell of appealing to youngsters. A roomful of computer cricket games would.

One obvious factor affecting membership and attendance is cost. Basic membership varies between £40 and £100 a year, and whether a county is at the top or bottom of this range bears little or no relationship to the facilities offered at its ground. At one end of the social scale, cost determines which club a spectator decides to support, particularly when that person is retired; I talked to a man who had switched from Northamptonshire, after a life-long allegiance, to Leicestershire because the latter was cheaper. At the upper end, some of the well-heeled cricket enthusiasts based in London and its environs are members of half-a-dozen clubs, and pick out the attractive fixtures from a big range of possibilities.

Someone who watches regularly should find annual membership of a club like Leicestershire - at £40 in year 2000 - a very good deal. Daily, pay-at-the-gate rates, generally between £8 to £10, are less so. They sound reasonable, being cheaper than any Premiership football tickets, and offering, potentially, four times the length of play. But then spectators may (and often do) sit around for hours during rain interruptions, are offered no guarantee of play, and (amazingly, when you stop to think about it) receive no refund should play not take place at all. Durham provided the best pay-at-the-gate bargain, at £5 a time - a sensible measure intended, presumably, to attract more casual visitors. None of the grounds I visited offered a four-day 'match ticket' bargain rate.

Spectators who attend English county cricket matches are almost without exception attentive and well informed - in contrast to many who flock to the Test matches to down their six pints of bitter and participate, unsteadily, in Mexican waves. Comment from the stands is well worth listening to, for its originality and humour, as well as its detailed knowledge of the game. This is not surprising, for many of the spectators have played the game with a passion, retiring to the stands only when old bones creak too noisily even for a place in the local reserve team.

In general, local cricket enthusiasms take precedence over national. Some spectators at county games take along transistor radios if a Test match is also in progress but, even on these occasions the relative inattention paid to the wider stage was striking. Regular attendance at one ground leads almost irresistibly to a state of parochialism. I began the season as someone who had previously attended the odd day of a match just to 'see some cricket' - perhaps a century from a top player. By the halfway stage of the 2000 season I was irretrievably a Leicestershire supporter, whose morale was linked to the ups and downs of his team. There is something gained in this, but also something lost. If, by some miracle of modern science, Jack Hobbs could be revived to turn out at Grace Road in a county fixture, I would want him to score a quick 50 and then get out.

Much pre-season speculation revolved around the new two-divisional championship and whether this would lead to more meaningful cricket. There was little doubt that it gingered things up for spectators. At all the grounds visited, you could overhear constant discussion about 'bonus points' and 'league positions'. The fervent burst of applause that greeted Somerset's fifth batting point in their last Taunton match spoke volumes, confirming as it did their First Division status (in a game that otherwise petered out to a draw). As for the players, one saw an astonishingly high level of commitment from most of them throughout the season, even when nothing - in terms of points or league position - was on offer.

A second constant was the 'local versus national' theme. Problems were created for those managing the national side by the local pride of county management and members, and the importance of registering points in a two-divisional set-up. The central contracts system, which removed the Test players from county sides for much of the season, was bitterly criticised in counties such as Yorkshire. Tough! As many pundits indicated, England's most successful season for decades coincided with the introduction of central contracts. I watched Yorkshire play twice, and was sorry not to see Darren Gough in either of the games. On the other hand I did see a battery of excellent Yorkshire seamers, one of whom, Matthew Hoggard, came all the way through to make the Test team, and the touring side for Pakistan. The massive gate receipts from England's test series victory over the West Indies were redistributed to make large contributions to county finances. Counties cannot have it both ways.

Appendix 1: The Leicestershire players

Leicestershire used a squad of 17 players for the 2000 season four-day championship matches. Players' ages, in brackets, are as on 1 April 2000.

Scott Boswell (26) played four games in his second season for Leicestershire and took a handful of wickets with his fast-medium bowling - seen at its best in Southampton.

Neil Burns (34). Among Leicestershire members there was season-long discussion of Paul Nixon's defection to Kent, rewarded - as many saw it - by his unusually poor season with the bat. Burns was drafted into the squad as the replacement keeper from his director of cricket post at minor county Buckinghamshire. He seemed understandably rusty in the early matches, but consistent performances - in all 16 games - soon won over spectators. Always good for between 30 and 40 runs in the middle order batting.

Carl Crowe (24) symbolised the plight of young English spinners. No sooner had Matthew Brimson retired than Leicestershire contracted Anil Kumble as their overseas player, and Crowe - who made his county debut in 1995 - was back to second-choice spinner. Given limited opportunities, he bowled well at Canterbury and outstandingly at Southampton, where his second innings 4 for 55 turned the match. With Kumble not contracted for 2001, Crowe might be given his head. Batted tenaciously (like all Leicestershire players) in the lower order. His best moment was making a difficult over-the-shoulder catch look easy at Southampton. His worst was getting sunstroke in Lancashire's second innings, on a Grace Road pitch that would, for once, have suited him.

John Dakin (27). Perhaps not a household name for non-Leicestershire supporters, but one of his county's most watchable players. In truth his presence can hardly be missed, and opposing spectators marvelled at his height, brute strength, and - ahem - weight. Had his best batting season for the county with an average of 44.7, but immediately after the award of his county cap, after seven seasons - following a marvellous century against Somerset - he was dropped, for a "general fitness overhaul". Took 12 wickets at 45.92, but generally bowled in short spells. His best moment showed with the grin on his face after hitting the winning runs against Somerset. Only played in nine of the 16 games, but Leicestershire always looked a better balanced side with him in the 11.

Philip DeFreitas (34), re-enlisted by his former county at an age when many cricketers are hanging up their boots, and had an extraordinary season characterised by all-out commitment. Took 33 wickets at 33.48 each, though early season bowling success dried up in later matches. His batting was a class act: 677 runs at 45.13 per innings (third in the county averages); belatedly promoted to seven in the order, he rarely failed to contribute and, above all, obviously enjoyed being at the crease. As his fast-medium bowling decelerates to medium-fast, he may turn into a batting (rather than bowling) all-rounder. Irrepressibly chirpy throughout the season. Performance against Lancashire at Grace Road suggested he had found an 'eternal youth' potion.

Aftab Habib (27) carried the Leicestershire batting throughout the season, scoring more than a thousand runs at an average of 49.43. His method is based upon a strong defence but, after playing himself in slowly, he scores with elegant strokes all round the wicket, occasionally unleashing a surprising straight six off spinners. Often caught in the slips, particularly after a resumption of play. His current first class average (44.4) puts him among the leading half-dozen English batsmen, and he looks every inch a Test match player. On the field, not a quick mover, but a very safe pair of hands. His best moment was kissing the stumps at Southampton after the ball had hit them but failed to dislodge a bail.

Anil Kumble (30) was Leicestershire's overseas player for the season. An excellent chance for the county's supporters to see the elegant, top-class Indian leg-spinner in action. He finished top of the bowling averages, with 45 wickets at 25.18 each, but did not dominate as expected - comparing unfavourably, for instance, with the season's performances from Saqlain and Warne, not to mention Tufnell, Giles and Salisbury. He was clearly disappointed with English pitches, and seemed reluctant to bowl long spells. Surprisingly, for a man with six first class hundreds, he finished bottom of the county batting averages, apparently unwilling to play himself in. Characteristic moment: met by small boys as he came off at a tea interval, signed one autograph before excusing himself with a charming smile saying: "I need a cup of tea".

Chris Lewis (31). Few famous players can have had a worse season. One off the bottom of the batting averages and fewer than 10 wickets, from a mere five games. Only his fielding attracted the right kind of attention. He left the county by mutual agreement at the end of the seas0on because of injury.

Darren Maddy (25). Indifferent season with the bat for this integral member of the Leicestershire side: 630 runs at an average of 26.41. Scored a century on the shirt-front pitch at Taunton, but his best was probably the second-innings 77 which made sure of victory against Durham. Fabulous fielding all over the playing area sets the tone for his county; took outstanding catches at slip, short-leg, and cover, and his spring-heeled run was instantly recognisable. Part-time bowling does not always come off, but was employed as a useful stand-breaker.

James Ormond (22). Already a major county player in his early twenties. With Kumble, the leading wicket-taker of the season - 44 wickets at 25.36 each. The only Leicestershire bowler with genuine pace, though he also took a wicket using spin at Guildford. Bowled a reliable line, though too many deliveries passed harmlessly outside off stump, including five of Leicestershire's first six in the season. He bowled sides out several times, though perhaps his most admirable performance was 4 for 122 in 34 overs at Old Trafford, during a mammoth Lancashire total. Rarely mentioned by the media as a future England player, yet his first-class average of 176 wickets at 24.2 each is bettered by only a couple of English bowlers. Spectacular fielder on the boundary, throwing his 14-stone frame into rolling stops.

Ben Smith (27). The Leicestershire vice-captain had a relatively poor season with the bat, averaging 30.5 from 22 innings. Confidently constructed centuries against Durham and Surrey stood out amongst many low scores. Took some fine catches in the slips. His slapstick re-entry onto the pitch at Taunton was straight from vaudeville. Imaginative captain on the two occasions when Wells was absent, particularly when keeping the same ball for 177 overs in Lancashire's huge innings at Grace Road.

Billy Stelling (30). Mystery package. Only played in the last, rain-ruined match of the season and promptly took five Kent wickets in an innings.

Darren Stevens (23). A one-pace batsman, and that pace is electric. Strike rate of 61.7 was only approached by De Freitas (59.0) - other Leicestershire batsmen were in the 40s or below. Stevens's contributions were eagerly awaited, but easily missed if you nipped out for a pint. Began the season as an opener, but settled at number six in the order. Management kept faith in their most entertaining batsman, though he scored only two 50s in 14 matches, and had a season's average of 21.7. Found all sorts of ways to get out, especially square of the wicket. Amid all the strokes, his whipped shot to the square-leg boundary off straight deliveries was a joy to behold.

Iain Sutcliffe (25). Left-handed opening bat, injured at the start of the season, but a regular for the last 10 matches. Adhesive and aggressive by turns, but a season's average of below 20 did not do him justice. Took numerous fine catches from suicidal silly mid-off/on positions.

Trevor Ward (32). Moved to Leicestershire after a respectable career with Kent, but things did not work out. Scarcely scored in the first seven matches, and was then dropped. His most memorable moment: almost decapitating umpire Constant with a fierce hook against Derbyshire. His worst moment was going like a train (for once) in the same innings, but the match ended.

Vince Wells (34). County captain, in his ninth season with the club. Leicestershire have profited with both bat and ball from Wells, who came to them in 1992 as Kent's deputy wicket-keeper. Hands-off captain, who leads by example, particularly when really needed - witness his bowling at Southampton. Typical all-rounder performance in year 2000, with 465 runs and 23 wickets. Effective, rustic stroke-player. Overdoes the bouncer when bowling. Stands at first slip for the quicks, but not the slows. Magic moments: three quick wickets against Yorkshire at Grace Road, as he wobbled the ball about alarmingly in overcast conditions.

Dominic Williamson (24). Only played two championship matches. Medium-pace bowling expensive, though he took a couple of crucial wickets with penetrating deliveries. His batting looked very accomplished.

Appendix 2: Statistics

Division One final table

	P	W	L	D	Bat	Bowl	Points
1. Surrey	16	9	2	5	44	41	213
2. Lancashire	16	7	1	8	35	42	193
3. Yorkshire	16	7	2	7	36	48	188*
4. Leicestershire	16	4	3	9	42	39	165
5. Somerset	16	2	4	10	41	40	145
6. Kent	16	4	4	8	18	42	140
7. Hampshire	16	3	9	4	20	48	112*
8. Durham	16	2	9	5	27	41	112
9. Derbyshire	16	2	6	8	19	44	111*

*Yorkshire, Hampshire and Derbyshire docked 8 points for poor pitches.

Leicestershire player County Championship averages

Batting

	M	I	NO	Runs	HS	Average
A. Habib	16	22	1	1038	172*	49.43
D. Williamson	2	4	2	95	47	47.50
PAJ DeFreitas	14	18	3	677	123*	45.13
JM Dakin	8	11	1	447	135	44.70
BF Smith	16	22	2	610	111*	30.50
DL Maddy	16	23	1	581	102	26.41
ND Burns	16	21	4	445	67*	26.18
VJ Wells	14	18	0	465	98	25.83
DI Stevens	14	20	0	434	78	21.70
IJ Sutcliffe	11	15	0	283	53	18.87
CD Crowe	7	7	1	100	30	16.67
SAJ Boswell	5	7	3	63	20	15.75
TR Ward	7	10	1	110	39	12.22
J Ormond	12	15	7	95	30*	11.88
CC Lewis	5	7	0	80	24	11.43
A Kumble	12	16	0	181	56	11.31

Bowling

	O	R	W	Average
A Kumble	498.3	1133	45	25.18
J Ormond	380.3	1116	44	25.36
VJ Wells	211.3	616	23	26.78
CD Crowe	148.3	364	12	30.33
PAJ DeFreitas	459.2	1105	33	33.48
JM Dakin	186.4	551	12	45.92

The Superb
Cricket Lore

Tim Rice - The Daily Telegraph

Now in its fourth Volume (10 issues per volume). *Cricket Lore* is a different magazine: subscription-based, limited-edition, A4 format, printed on very high quality paper, detailed and considered articles, and few advertisments. *Cricket Lore* deals at length with many aspects of cricket - its history is researched; the contemporary game discussed; opinion surveys undertaken; players and 'officials' interviewed. *Cricket Lore* is already a 'collectable' and has established the highest reputation as these quotes from readers demonstrate:

"Let me recommend to readers the quality of Cricket Lore."
EW Swanton, The Cricketer International

"A valuable amalgam of cricket literature
and comment on the way the game is going"
David Foot, Prize-winning cricket author and journalist

"Cricket Lore brings an historical perspective to contemporary issues"
David Rayvern Allen - Author & official biographer of John Arlott

" A cricket connoisseur's delight ... Cricket Lore has the appearance
and, more to the point, the substance of an enterprise of merit ...
Full of interest, well-written and attractively illustrated,
its contents repay attention."
CW Porter, Editor of *Journal of the Cricket Society*

"Hill's quality periodical, Cricket Lore, continues to fascinate"
Tim Rice, The Daily Telegraph

"Cricket Lore treats history seriously and that means
with an eye to its contemporary relevance.
Under Richard Hill's robust editorship, cricket is revealed as
a great continuum in the sporting life of the nation."
Simon Rae, broadcaster & author of the acclaimed *WG Grace A Life*

"The outstanding Cricket Lore is the finest magazine of its type."
Bernard Whimpress, Curator of the Adelaide Oval Museum

Contributors include: Eric Midwinter, Frank Tyson, Peter Wynne-Thomas, Stephen Chalke, David Foot, Peter Hartland, Simon Rae, Roderick Easdale, Tim Heald, Roger Heavens, Keith Sandiford, Bernard Whimpress, Christopher Sandford, Brian Bassano, G Derek West, Neil Cole, Richard Parry, Barry Rickson, David Seymour, Bill Lewis, Barry Nicholls, Neville Turner etc.

You may sample a copy of *Cricket Lore* at £3.50 - Please forward Cheques to:

Cricket Lore 22 Grazebrook Road London N16 0HS

Tel: 020 8800 0131   email clore@globalnet.co.uk

Rugby League Analysis, History & Vision

A new national Rugby League magazine published twice a year.

Third edition (Spring 2001) now out, with articles on:
- **Cumberland's Game** by Harry Edgar
- **All for the Union? Trade union organisation in rugby league** by Michael O'Hare and Braham Dabscheck
- **Truth on display at Twickenham** by Tony Collins
- **1985 and all that** by Phil Melling
- **Andy Gregory** by Bill Lythgoe
- **Changing the rules** by Geoff Lee
- **Rugby league poetry**
- **Book reviews, obituaries** and much more
- And introducing our new cartoon: **Grubber**

New Writing on Rugby League

To order a copy post free, send a cheque for £2.00 to:
London League Publications, PO Box 10441, London E14 0SB.
(no credit card orders).
Free booklist of our sports books now available.

Our Game is also available from Sportspages (London & Manchester), The
Sports Bookshop, Cardiff and Smiths of Wigan.

Rugby's Class War
Bans, boot money and parliamentary battles
By David Hinchliffe M.P.

Rugby's Class War is the untold story of the climax of the historic battle between the two codes of rugby as Rugby Union finally succumbed to open professionalism.

It is a hard hitting account of the way the bigotry, elitism and hypocrisy underpinning Rugby Union's long-standing attempts to outlaw the separate sport of Rugby League were finally challenged and confronted.

Five years on from Union's decision to openly pay its players and from League's controversial formation of its Super League, the book analyses the revolutionary changes in both codes and examines the prospects for one united form of rugby.

This book is essential reading for followers of both Rugby League and Rugby Union who are interested in the history and the future of both codes.

Rugby's Class War is written by David Hinchliffe, the Labour M.P. who was at the forefront of the parliamentary campaign to bring Union's discrimination against League to an end.

Foreword by **Stuart Evans** (Neath and Wales Rugby Union, St Helens Rugby League)

Introduction by **Harry Edgar** (former editor of *Open Rugby*)

Published in October 2000 at £9.75; special offer to readers of this book: order your copy for £9.00 post free. Order from:
London League Publications Ltd, PO Box 10441, London E14 0SB.
Cheques payable to London League Publications Ltd, no credit card orders.